THE FADED STAIN

THE FADED STAIN

A MEMOIR

By Sheila Patricia Ingram

To my beloved daughters, Nichole Dawn, Pache' Collette, DeAnjolie' Christina

And to every soul who has ever tried to outrun their own shadow.

You are holding the true story of how chaos became my inheritance. This is not a book of excuses; it is a **detailed map** for navigating out of the trenches. It is a testament to the fact that the cycle of trauma can be broken, even in the very place where a total breakdown once stood.

Where there was once a stain, there is now a story of survival.

Introduction: The Trench

The cold pavement bit through my thin clothes. The weight of the handcuffs was the physical manifestation of the despair I had been outrunning for two decades. I was Sheila, the singer, the star who had graced the stage of Studio 54, and yet here I was, kneeling on the side of the New Jersey Turnpike, arrested, freezing, and utterly broken.

The humiliation was a greater pain than the winter air. When they drove me to the small-town courthouse and then led me into the female jail, I was numb. But numbness is temporary. When I woke up the next morning, my fever was high, and I was violently ill. I was surrounded by hundreds of desperate women, and I was sinking into a trench of despair that felt deeper and darker than any stage light I had ever known.

How did I get here?

I was a seventeen-year-old widow who had run from my husband's death straight into the chaos of the entertainment world. I had chased the applause to silence the screams of my past. I had tried to fix my father's rage, overcome my mother's disappointment, and outrun the quiet, growing resentment of my daughters. The Stain—my lifelong trauma of loss, guilt, and fear—had finally won.

This memoir is the map of that failure, and the testament to my ultimate freedom. It is the story of The Stain—a wound that came in three distinct parts:

The Inherited Burden of my chaotic childhood.

The Immediate Crush of the murder of my young husband, Wayne.

The Self-Imposed Consequence of my subsequent gilded escape and emotional distance from my children.

I share the truth of the dark path I took so that you may understand that no wound is too deep to heal, and no collapse is too great for divine intervention. My story begins not on this cold jail floor, but decades earlier, in the moment a bullet slammed shut the door on my greatest joy and started me on a run that nearly cost me everything.

This is the story of how the old passed away, how the seeds of a new creation were planted in the quiet despair of a dingy jail cell, and how that life finally broke through the soil on a church floor, where the blood of forgiveness spoke a better word than the blood of vengeance.

A Note from the Author:

The "Heart-to-Heart"

To You, My Reader,

I want you to know that this is more than just a collection of chapters. It is a journey of restoration that took me a lifetime to reach, but I knew I had to go there because of the complexities, the ups, the downs, and the turnarounds of my life. I realized that no one could tell my story for me. I had to speak my own truth in the rhythm of how I lived it, the rhythm of how I sing, and the rhythm of how I give it to you.

As you read, you will run into spaces and places where you can stop, pause, and reflect. You might want to jot down something you need to remember, or you may choose to use your own paper—whatever you decide, this journey is yours.

From the depths of the "Trenches" to the height of the **Kabod Room**—that sacred place where God's manifested glory shows up—this story is from my heart to yours. It was not written for me alone; I have shared my life and the life of my family so you can see that there is no shame in your past. There is no shame in anything you have had to walk through, live through, or where you might be right now. There is only Victory, if you choose to do the work and walk through it.

Interspersed within this memoir, you will find sacred spaces to pause and document your own journey. As you witness the fading of my stains, I invite you to pick up your own pen. These are jewels for the weary and a map for the soul ready to move from pain to power, and from power to Victory. **Your story matters, too. Let's just keep it movin'.** *With Love,* **Sheila Patricia Ingram**

HEARTS WITHOUT WALLS:

THE MOVEMENT

Hearts Without Walls is a global mandate for radical restoration founded by Sheila Ingram, LPC. This is a movement dedicated to the Restoration of the Human Soul—breaking down the internal defenses built by trauma, grief, and the "stains" of the past.

We believe that no matter how deep the mark, the rhythm of your life can be restored. Through the Hearts Without Walls Bridge, we provide "Oxygen" for those who have been suffocating in the trenches of their history.

The Mission:

BREATHE: Providing the emotional and mental space for resuscitation.

BRIDGE: Connecting the wounded soul back to its purpose and potential and the Original Intent.

BUILD: Establishing a legacy no longer defined by the stain, but by the strength of the survivor.

Erasing the Stain. Restoring the Rhythm. Keeping it Movin'. www.IRGoutreach.org

HEARTS WITHOUT WALLS
INGRAM RESTORATION
GLOBAL OUTREACH INC.
HEARTS WITHOUT WALLS

"Plus, special Reflections, Spiritual Anchors, and The Rehab Experience throughout the journey."

The Original Intent: 1969

Before the Stain

"It was 1969. I was a mother with my first daughter. Wayne had become a staple around the house. My mother wasn't too excited because Wayne was five years older than me, but she couldn't deny the respect he had for me. Before Wayne, I was a young schoolgirl making a name for myself. I decided to run for school secretary and took off with it. I knocked on the principal's door with a vision for a 'Movie Day' and brought in Marlon Brando's *on the Waterfront*. I wanted to introduce the students to a different genre.

Those were the days Beverly, and I spent weekends buying material and cutting out patterns for our dresses. We would buy shoes and dye them to match our vibrant colors. Life was good. Wayne was encouraging me to keep up with school, but he wasn't a fan of my desire to be a singer. I would laugh at the fear on his face—fear that the music might take me away from him.

Before Wayne, I would sing at community events and hit Latin dances. I was the youngest, the 'tag-along' my mother forced on my sister, but I was mature and I fit right in. When that music pulled us in, we would dance for hours. Every weekend there we went to the Apollo Theater. I was mesmerized, in a trance, closing my eyes and seeing myself on that stage. Even when security put us out, we'd run to the back, and the ushers would let us back in. We even became the fan club for The Manhattans—that was the highlight of our lives, performing on stages with them. We were having the time of our young lives, never imagining the shift that was about to happen."

Chapter 1: The Name of the Wound

(The Origin of the Stain)

"He heals the brokenhearted and binds up their wounds" Psalm147:3

I was talking with my youngest daughter about the complex, painful distance that had settled between me and her older sisters. We were in a restaurant, and the conversation was tense, full of the unsaid emotions that had defined our family life.

As we spoke, she did something that stopped me cold. She picked up the ketchup bottle and began carefully pouring the thick, red sauce into a base of white, creamy dipping sauce on her plate. It looked repulsive, and mesmerizing, all at once.

"Do you see what that looks like?" she asked, without looking up.

I stared at the spreading color. The red was bleeding outward, contaminating the white, clean background. "It looks like a stain," I answered.

She looked at me, her gaze piercing. "That's what happened with you and my sisters, they received the stain that you had."

In that single, sharp sentence, my lifelong trauma was finally named. My youngest daughter, the one who had grown up in the years after my life of chaotic running had stopped—gave me the title for my memoir.

The Immediate Crush

The Stain arrived in the most cruel, unexpected way possible, slamming the door on the season of joy.

It was January 13, 1972, and the world had just cracked open to let in new life. I had just delivered our second daughter via an emergency C-section. This birth, which was perilous due to the baby being turned and breech—a major problem for both of us—was physically tumultuous, just like the circumstances surrounding our first daughter's arrival when I was fifteen. However, with Wayne, my **husband of four months**, by my side—the man I truly loved and who anchored our family—this moment felt like a **stable start**, a chance to overcome the chaos, despite the physical danger.

My mother later told me that just before he left, he and she stood together, looking at our new daughter. He was beaming with pride, saying, "Look, she looks just like me." The doctors had put me into recovery after the serious C-section, and because my status wasn't totally stable and I desperately needed rest, they wouldn't allow him to stay. He kissed me goodbye, saying he was just running home to quickly change his clothes and take a shower, promising to be right back. He was beaming before he left.

The Unthinkable News

I was lying in the clean, sterile white of the hospital room when my father walked in. The C-section had left me exhausted and relieved. The room was quiet, sacred—the birthplace of hope.

But my father's demeanor instantly shattered the peace. He was alone, and he looked shifty. Worse, I recognized the strange, bottled-up anxiety he wore when he'd been drinking alcohol, a look that signaled he needed courage just to stand there. In that moment, the Inherited Stain of my childhood fused with the Immediate Stain of my loss.

He came close to the bed, but his words were so low I could barely hear them.

"Daddy, I can't hear you. What happened?" I asked, confused. The tension in the room was thicker than the bandages around my waist.

He repeated only one word, his eyes darting away from mine: "Wayne… Wayne."

"Wayne what?" The panic started to rise up in my chest, hot and fast. I knew, somehow, before he said it, that the look on his face something terrible had happened. "He leaned in, and I could barely hear him, but the words hit me like a physical blow. 'Wayne is dead. He's gone.'"

***

"But before the darkness of that day, there was the light of our 'Yes.' My mother had made it clear to Wayne that he was going to make an honest woman out of me, and he was overjoyed—he had always wanted me to be his wife. We planned a 'Rainbow Wedding' with eight bridesmaids, a beautiful, huge celebration of the life we were building.

The night before we said, 'I do,' the rain was pouring over the bridge. A five-car collision sent my head into the windshield and left Wayne with a broken arm. Instead of a rehearsal dinner, the entire wedding party spent the night in the hospital. The next morning, I stood at the altar with my head full of broken glass in my head and my husband's arm in a cast. We were legally married. For the first time, I didn't have to race the sun home; I was a wife.

That glass stayed in my head for months and years after—the scars were a physical imprint of that night. I chose to have my daughters at Roosevelt Hospital in Manhattan because I wanted the best for them. Wayne was my protector, my provider, and my husband. He was God-sent. That is why the devastation of his murder, on the very day our youngest was born, didn't just break my heart—it shifted my entire world into the stain."

***

I screamed. It was a primal, ugly sound that tore out of my body. I totally lost it. The shock of the news slammed against the fresh incision from the C-section, and the physical pain merged with the spiritual pain. My body convulsed, a total collapse. I wanted my mother. She was the one who was supposed to anchor me.

I demanded they push my hospital bed, tubes and all, out into the corridor so I could call her. The doctors looked confused and angry, wondering how my father had even made it past the nurses who were under explicit orders: No one was to tell me the news yet. My mother would tell me. Everyone on the ward knew what had happened. They had been protecting me because of the surgery, afraid of how my mental state would handle the news. The truth was, I was too sick to even hold my newborn daughter in the aftermath.

But the words had been spoken, the protection was gone, and the damage was done. My father's betrayal of my mother's order, fueled by his need for a drink to face a tragedy, permanently engraved the trauma.

I was seventeen years old, a mother of two, and a widow.

 I felt the Stain show up in my life—a deep, dark mark of trauma and guilt that clung to my heart. It was a searing mark: If only he hadn't left…. If only the *button hadn't popped off…. If only he hadn't argued….* Wayne's death, rooted in a senseless act of violence, sent me on a detour that took over half of my life to recover from.

I learned to run. I would run from anything that required accountability. I would run from anything that required commitment. I would run from anything that required me to be totally honest. To get a handle on the deep dark hole I was in, I threw myself into the chaotic fast lane of my singing career. I did not leave Harlem, but this immersion into the destructive environment of nightclubs and after-hours clubs became my first attempt at the great escape. I was a 17-year-old widow trying to outrun a lifetime of pain, spinning into a space of depression and insecurity.

Counselor's Insight: The Anatomy of the Escape

When trauma is too heavy for a seventeen-year-old heart to carry, the mind looks for an exit. For me, that exit was the neon lights and the music of the nightclubs. We often think of "running" as a physical act, but in my counseling practice, I've learned that running is a state of the soul. We run into careers, into relationships, into "masking" our way through the day so we don't have to feel the weight of the "Stain."

The Kabod Question: If *you stopped running right now—just for a moment—what is the one truth you are most afraid would catch up to you?*

____

____

The Hearts Without Walls Bridge: When the truth catches up to us, our first instinct is to build a wall—to hide behind the career, the mask, or the neon lights. But the movement of **Hearts Without Walls** starts with a single, honest breath. It starts by inviting the One who ordered your steps even when you were running away from Him. If you are tired of the "Gilded Escape," take a breath. This is your **Oxygen**.

Oxygen: A Heart Without Walls Prayer

Lord thank you for this day, I know it is by your grace that I rise today. I will rejoice and be glad on this beautiful day I awake to. I know that this day is a new day. Every day is an opportunity

to be more like you. My steps are ordered by you Lord. May I be sensitive to hear what you are saying to me as I seek you in my prayer time. Lord, I pray that I be mindful of my actions and choices I make on this day. Lord gives me strength and grace to take the high road when I am challenged in my walk.

Help me make decisions you will be pleased with.

Amen

Chapter 2: The Inherited Stain

"I will restore to you the years that the swarming locust has eaten" Joel 2:25

The Double-Edged Birth

I sat in the hospital chair, staring out the window at a world that looked the same as it had yesterday, yet was entirely unrecognizable. I felt empty—not just from the surgery, but from the soul-crushing realization that my newborn daughter would never know the man who gave her his name.

This was the "Double-Edged Birth." In one hand, I held the miracle of new life; in the other, I held the heavy, cold weight of a sudden death. The hospital room felt like a vacuum. I was surrounded by the sounds of a busy ward—nurses whispering, babies crying—but I was in a trance of despair. The Stain was already beginning to seep into the fabric of my motherhood. I looked at my baby and, for a fleeting, terrifying moment, I saw the tragedy instead of the child. I had to learn how to be a parent while I was still essentially a child myself, reeling from a blow I couldn't understand.

The Stain that arrived with Wayne's death was not the first trauma I had known; it was just the darkest. Long before I knew what trauma was, I was living with the Inherited Stain—the quiet, constant trauma of my father's alcoholism.

I grew up feeling shame and embarrassment, but unlike the "secret" my mother desperately tried to keep, our neighbors knew. They knew which nights our house was quiet—the nights we could breathe— and they knew when the chaos had returned, because on many other nights, there was yelling, screaming, and the desperate sound of doors slamming when he came home intoxicated. The knowledge that the outside world knew our inner turmoil deepened the mark of the Stain on my young soul.

But we learned to survive. My siblings and I learned to hold our heads up high when we walked the streets of Harlem, acting like everything was okay. We wore masks of composure, afraid that if we let our guard down, the truth of our broken home would swallow us whole. We became masters of the facade.

My father was a good man, a hardworking man, but when he drank, he became a completely different person. He had a much different, and often easier, relationship with my older sister. There was a connection between them that was always obvious to me. Because of this connection, she was the one he would listen to when the madness began. It was my sister who had the ability to get my father to stop the chaos.

But he treated me differently. I knew he loved me, but later in life, I came to the heartbreaking conclusion that I reminded him of my mother, who everyone could see I had a strong connection with. This made me a target for his complex, alcohol-fueled emotions.

The Sound of Shattered Laughter

I became the Peacemaker in our home, the one who tried to fix and manage the unpredictable atmosphere. I felt responsible for the feelings of everyone around me, especially my father's mood and my mother's distress. I always tried to do everything perfectly so I wouldn't add any extra stress to the house. I was constantly walking on eggshells, afraid of what might happen when he came home. But one night, the protective shield I carried shattered. I remember we were all together—my sister, my brother, and I—and my father came home under the influence. He began reciting something loudly, puffing out his chest, but what he was reciting was wrong. His drunken delivery was so off-key that the three of us burst into uncontrolled laughter. It was a release, a moment of childhood innocence reclaiming the space the alcohol had stolen.

He didn't like it. He didn't like being the butt of the joke. He spun around, and out of all of us laughing, he turned to me. He walked right past my older sister and my brother, singled me out, and he hit me.

The laughter stopped instantly. It was replaced by a ringing silence and the shock that freezes a child's heart. I have never forgotten that moment. It wasn't just the pain of the blow; it was the sting of the injustice. Why me? Why did I have to pay for the shared moment of relief?

This taught me a dangerous lesson: that I was responsible for fixing the broken things in the world, starting with my father. This need to fix and control everything—to be the rescuer—would follow me into my adult relationships, manifesting as co-dependency. The Inherited Stain had taken root long before 1972, and it was a sickness that dictated my every move.

The Burden of the Savior:

Codependency Takes Root. The Peacemaker role intensified once my mother gained the courage to separate from and later divorced my father. While the screaming stopped, the household chaos simply changed.

My mother began to host parties, and the people who frequented our home were not always the

best influences. The burden of protection immediately transferred from shielding my mother from my father's rage to shielding her from the external world. I took on the responsibility of guarding my mother's money and watching over her to ensure her safety and financial security among the less-than-reputable crowd. I became her protector and her constant lookout.

This was a profound shift: the child became the parent. This deep, intense need to be the Savior—to fix, protect, and be accountable for the well-being and stability of the person closest to me—spilled catastrophically into my adulthood I became codependent, unconsciously getting in relationships with men who were emotionally unavailable, required fixing, or needed protection, ensuring I could always retain my familiar role as the indispensable rescuer.

This pattern continued for decades, linking me to the very chaos I was trying to escape. After my spiritual awakening, I recognized this deeply embedded spirit of codependency as a major part of The Stain's control.

It was only through dedicated Christian counseling that I was delivered from this lifelong pattern, allowing me to finally build relationships based on mutual respect rather than the constant, exhausting need to save another person.

The Triumph of the Provider

As I carried the weight of this protective role, **I was also a witness to my mother's incredible triumph and resilience. She found her voice, cleared the house of the lingering dysfunction, and focused intensely on her career. A relentless worker, she dedicated herself to the United States Post Office, where she rose to a position of indispensable competence—one that no one could work without because of her intelligence and intensity.**

I watched her provide for me, my sister, and my brother. We wanted for nothing, and there was nothing she wouldn't do for us. Her success was a powerful, tangible demonstration of strength and commitment, teaching me a complex truth: The source of my codependency (the fear of her vulnerability) was intertwined with the object of my deepest admiration (her unwavering power as a provider). This paradox made my dedication to her safety—and the subsequent codependency it instilled in me—feel not like a flaw, but a necessity.

CHAPTER 3: The Price of Perfection

Scripture Anchor: *"But the Lord said unto Samuel, Look not on his countenance, or on the height of his stature; because I have refused him: for the Lord seeth not as man seeth; for man looketh on the outward appearance, but the Lord looketh on the heart."* — 1 Samuel 16:7

The Opening: The Weight of the Mask The weight of the stain didn't start with the bullet; it started years earlier when I was fifteen years old. Because of the pressure and the chaos of my childhood, because I was trying so desperately to be the perfect Peacemaker, I was already sinking into a deeper darkness. When I became pregnant at fifteen, I felt like I had literally broken my mother's heart into pieces.

I remember her scream—raw, shocked, and laced with self-blame. "What have I done?" she cried. She felt guilty, and I felt terrible, drowning in a shame that consumed me for days. I stayed in my room, afraid to face the disappointment of the woman I loved more than anyone.

One day, she called me out. It was one of the hardest things I ever had to do—facing her. She asked me to sit down, and the first thing she said crushed me.

"You are no longer Lump-Dump," she declared, referring to the nickname of affection everyone knew me by. "You are now Sheila. You have laid down when I told you about the birds and the bees, and now you are a woman."

The carefree girl, the protected "Lump-Dump," was gone in a single sentence. But then she pivoted with that fierce maternal strength: "We are just going to have us a baby, and it's not the end of the world. You will hold your head up, and we will deal with this together. Just promise me you will finish school."

COUNSELOR'S INSIGHT: THE MIRAGE OF THE ERASER

When the shame of a past trauma feels like an indelible mark, the human instinct is to try and "erase" it with perfection. We believe that if we become the perfect mother, the perfect professional, or the perfect provider, the old "Stain" will simply vanish.

But perfection is a mirage. It does not erase the wound; it only masks the pain while we run toward a horizon that never gets closer. You cannot "perform" your way out of a "Stain." You must "process" your way through it.

YOUR TURN TO BREATHE

The Six Layers of the Stain Identify which of these feels the heaviest in your spirit today:

1. **The Literal Stain** (The physical evidence of the trauma)

2. **The Moral Stain** (The weight of "What have I done?")

3. **The Social Stain** (The fear of what the world will say)

4. **The Emotional Stain** (The constant, quiet despair)

5. **The Professional Stain** (The fear that your past ruins your future)

6. **The Generational Stain** (The inherited burden from your lineage)

In the space below, name the layer you are ready to lay at the feet of Jesus today:

THE HEARTS WITHOUT WALLS PRAYER

Lord, we thank You that You see us—not for the mistakes we've made, and not for the masks we wear, but for the daughters and sons You created. We pray for every heart reading these words that feels the exhaustion of trying to be "perfect".

Chapter 4: The Gilded Escape

(The Nightclub Persona)

"Where shall I go from your Spirit? Or where shall I flee from your presence?"-Psalm 139—the Gilded Escape.

I immersed myself in the destructive environment of nightclubs and after-hours spots, creating a brilliant, chaotic detour that became my existence. Music wasn't just my career; it was my oxygen mask. I thought that if I kept moving, kept singing, and kept the audience enjoying my performance, I could outrun the seventeen-year-old widow staring out the hospital window. I was traveling the world, but I was carrying the same heavy luggage in my soul. Even as the crowd screamed my name, I was still Lump Dump inside, waiting for the other shoe to drop. The music was loud enough to drown out the screams of my mother's voice from the past and the silence of my own present grief.

The Persona of Sheila Ingram: The Peak

I didn't just sing at one prestigious venue; I sang at almost every major five-star club and restaurant in New York City. Before my life took its chaotic turn, the name Sheila Ingram was synonymous with high-end, legitimate entertainment. I performed at legendary venues like the Riverboat, the Copacabana, and, yes, the incredibly prestigious Studio 54 "...My mentor and music teacher, Reggie, was responsible for these incredible opportunities, believing in me and encouraging me more than anyone else.

One day I was standing on the corner of 115th and Lenox, and the next I was walking into a hangar and boarding a Learjet to California to sing background for Lou Rawls. It was incredible, but on the road, things got heavy..."

"I was on the corner of 115th and Lenox one day, and the next day I was walking into a hangar and boarding a Learjet to California to sing background for Lou Rawls. It was incredible. But on the road, things got heavy. Two of the other singers asked me into their room and wanted me to do things I was against doing intimacy I wasn't into. Because I refused, they took offense.

They treated me bad from that point on. When we got back to New York for the Budweiser parade with the Clydesdale horses, I was so excited for my friends to see me on Broadway. But those girls called me to a restaurant and told me a lie—that Lou didn't need me anymore. My heart fell to my stomach. I had children to feed; I depended on that paycheck. They betrayed me just to get me out of the way."

The Mink and the Mask

"When we left that restaurant, I didn't even want to get in the car with them, but they convinced me. As we walked into the garage, men in ski masks with double-barrel shotguns stepped out. They put those guns in our backs and marched us to the lower level.

I was standing there in my mink coat and my mink hat, telling them to take my jewelry, take my clothes—just don't hurt us. They didn't want my stuff; they were there to rob the garage. I got home and all I could do was cry, cry, cry. The betrayal of those 'sisters' and the terror of those guns was almost more than I could take. The Stain is a quiet passenger; it doesn't need a ticket to follow you across borders. As I toured the world, I began to realize that my "Impediment" was actually my "Testimony," though I didn't have the spiritual language for it yet. I was dispensing informal wisdom in dressing rooms and hotels, helping other performers navigate their pain while mine was still an open wound.

The pressure of being the perfect performer for the world and the "perfect" mother from a distance was a crushing weight. My children were growing up, and the Stain was trickling over into their lives, fueled by my absence and my own unresolved grief. The music was beautiful, but the silence between the songs was becoming unbearable. I was a seasoned traveler who had seen the world, but I was still a stranger to my own peace. I was running toward a horizon that never seemed to get any closer, and the "Gilded Escape" was beginning to feel like a marathon with no finish line.

Even in my rehearsals, the Stain followed me, leaving me down in my spirit. But the roar of instant validation from these legendary stages silenced the Stain briefly. Only huge stars had the opportunity to grace stages like these. The feeling of accomplishment had no comparison to the other clubs I had played so far. My family was there to anchor the moment: my brother was a huge support and came to all my shows, and my mother was front and center, often threatening her friends to come, a hilarious joke we still speak of today.

I walked to the center of the stage, dressed in tailored gowns, completely transformed into Sheila Ingram. The venues were electric—mirrored walls, flashing strobe lights, and a crowd that was a glittering sea of diamonds and velvet. The spotlight was a cone of searing heat that created an impenetrable barrier between me and the world of grief and guilt. The crowd was electric and so supportive, cheering me on as a new artist.

The After-Hours Crash (The Low)

The gilded lights of the world stage eventually dimmed, leading me into the "Trench." This was the world of after-hours clubs and smoky rooms where the night never seemed to end. I was looking for a refuge, but I found a trap. The adrenaline of the hustle was the only thing that made me feel alive, but it was a "Gilded Escape" that was rapidly losing its luster. I was no longer just singing for the joy of it; I was singing to survive the darkness that was closing in.

When the moment began to shift back to my reality of going uptown, guilt lurked in the corner of my soul. I could not give myself a moment to feel one hundred percent full of joy because I knew that once I started my way back to Harlem, my emotions were going to shift.

The decline began the instant the microphone was turned off. With my elegant clothing gone, the crushing weight of reality returned. This is when the real escape began: the transition to the after-hours clubs. This was a step down—a desperate attempt to maintain the chaos and the income.

If Studio 54 was champagne and spectacle, the after-hours was a desperate attempt to maintain the chaos and the income. I had a choice of which after-hours club to go to, and the decor of the spots I found myself in was always nice, but the clientele was often dangerous: high-end dealers, business owners, entertainers, and "regulars" who had to be known for the safety of those present. I had done nothing on a low standard; even my after-hours escape maintained a high-stakes, exclusive clientele.

The Three-Set Hell

I was often booked to sing multiple "spots," as we called them. One night, I was incredibly depressed and was asked to do three sets. I immediately wanted to refuse—three sets at an after-hours club. That was insane to me—but I took the gig because I had to pay our household bills.

On this night, a famous singer, who we will call Kubba G, was scheduled to perform. He and his group were stars with hit records, and he knew my name because I was "Harlem's little star." The owner wanted him to go on first, and he felt it belittled him to open for me. The entire night was a night of hell. He was obnoxious and rude.

I went into the bathroom and began to cry. I hated being in this position, having to do three exhausting sets and leaving early in the morning to go home and not being able to function as a parent. Yes, I was providing, but I was once again paying a big price. Thank God for my mother.

Adjusting to being a widow was wearing me down. I was still crying for Wayne, but no one knew. They saw my actions—the successful singer—and not my broken heart. The music was loud enough to drown out the screams of my mother's voice from the past and the silence of my present grief, but the after-hours chaos was slowly draining the last reserves of my strength.

The Cost of Running

This escape cost me the only thing more valuable than my peace: my relationships with my daughters.

Between the need to work as a singer to provide for them and the desperate need to run away from the Stain, I created a distance I have never fully recovered from. I wanted to be the perfect mother, the strong rock my own mother had been, but I didn't know how. Trauma engulfed me, and all I could think about was my loss. I just wanted Wayne to return so I could have help.

My mother was the absolute parent who took the load off of me. By this time, she was full of joy to do it, seeing it as an opportunity to have a do-over, to clear up her own shame about her past parenting. She made sure we had what we needed. But her love couldn't bridge the gap I created. The roar of the crowd masked my tears, the smoke of the club hid my shame, and my mother's love was the only thing that kept the Stain from consuming my children entirely. I was a star in public but a failure in the home, and the silent resentment of my daughters was the true price of the Gilded Escape.

The Unspoken Trauma: The Deep Root of Abandonment

Now that I am older, I recognize that the central, corrosive theme running through my entire life was the constant trauma of abandonment. It did not just happen once; it was a repeated pattern that deeply shaped my survival mechanisms:

First, the Inherited Abandonment from my father, whose emotional presence was stolen by alcoholism, teaching me that love was conditional and unreliable. Second, the Crushing Abandonment when Wayne was brutally killed, leaving me a widow and a mother at seventeen, facing life without my anchor.

Third, the Betrayal Abandonment when the father of my youngest daughter left, confirming the pattern that the men I depended on would ultimately disappear.

Finally, the Reciprocal Abandonment I felt when my own daughters, in pain, created a distance and silence that felt like a rejection.

Because this pattern was so deeply ingrained, I developed a critical survival mechanism: I tend to preemptively abandon the relationship, or build an impenetrable wall of perfection and self-sufficiency, before anyone can get close enough to leave me again. My role as the "peacemaker" was really a form of control, and my "Gilded Escape" was the ultimate act of self-abandonment, running from intimacy to avoid inevitable loss. This constant fear of being left was the silent engine that drove my chaos for decades.

Counselor's Insight: Identifying the Engine

In Chapter 2, I shared the four types of abandonment that built the "engine" of my chaos. In my practice, I find that many people are being driven by engines they didn't build—engines of fear, rejection, or addiction inherited from a house in their own past. The good news of **Joel 2:25** is that God doesn't just fix the engine; He replaces the fuel. He restores the years that the "locusts" of abandonment tried to eat away.

The Kabod Reflection: Which *of the four abandonments (Inhabited, Crushing, Betrayal, or Reciprocal) resonates most with your story?*

- *If you could name the "Silent Engine" driving your choices today, what would you call it? (Fear, Perfectionism, Anger, or Isolation?)*

____

____

____

____

The Hearts Without Walls Bridge When you name the engine, you take away its power to drive you in secret. But you cannot just leave the seat empty; you must invite a new Driver. At **Hearts Without Walls**, we believe that the only way to stop the "Gilded Escape" is to start an internal conversation with the One who never leaves. If you feel like your goals are impossible because your past is too heavy, take a breath. This is your **Oxygen**.

The Oxygen: A Heart Without Walls Prayer "Holy Spirit, thank you for coming and being an Encourager when I need You the most. There are assignments, dreams, and courageous goals in my spirit that seem impossible to bring forth. But thanks be to God, the Holy Spirit is here with me to encourage me. There is nothing that is impossible with You. There is nothing I cannot accomplish. The Lord is with me. I know you are my Shepherd and I trust you, Lord. I know you will provide for my every need, so I declare today that nothing is impossible and all things are working together for my good. I have the victory and I shall see the manifestation of Your marvelous plans for my life.

THE GILDED ESCAPE

A "Gilded Escape" is the act of covering one's internal trauma with external excellence. It is the brilliant, golden distraction of success—the applause, the spotlights, and the prestige—that we use to outrun the shadow of our past. It looks like a victory to the world, but it is a chaotic detour for the soul. It is "gilded" because it is shiny on the outside, but underneath, the "Stain" remains untouched.

CHAPTER 5: The Daughters Silence

Scripture Anchor: "All your children shall be taught of the Lord, and great shall be the peace of your children." — Isaiah 54:13

The Price of the Gilded Escape The glitter of the nightclub stage offered a brilliant distraction, yes, the Stain has had its way with me and my children, but we Win. For the Stain has faded off my mind, The Gilded Escape was a beautiful, chaotic lie. The music career I had hoped would save me was simply draining the last reserves of my strength. The shell of "Sheila Ingram, the Singer" was running on fumes, and the Stain was preparing to claim its ultimate victory. Things were really slowing down. I wasn't getting many calls or bookings for performances. At this point, I had already been on the Apollo Stage three times, yet I found myself being booked at the same clubs repeatedly. The thrill of it all was almost non-existent. I thought by now I would have a record deal, but the promised future was simply not arriving. Things began to close in on me. I thought about moving to Italy, a place far away where I knew people who I was sure would help me, but as quickly as the thought arrived, I let it go. I still desperately wanted to repair my relationship with my children, so I knew running farther away wasn't the answer.

I was so tired. People would remind me that I had already lived the life of a forty-year-old woman, being a widow and a mother so young. I truly felt down; I was running out of steam. I went deeper inside of the lonely cave within me, yet I continued to smile. My anxiety was obvious to me, but I had a way of keeping away from people when I was deep in that type of depression.

But the real price of my "Gilded Escape" was being paid in full by the people I loved most: my children. As I ran from my own pain.

I inadvertently created a new layer of trauma for them. The "Stain" convinced me that the best way to protect them was to provide for them, and that meant pouring my energy into a career that kept me physically distant and emotionally absent.

They were in the safest place with my mother, the Rock of our family—but their own mother was only present in snapshots between shows. Don't get me wrong I was present for important moments like school functions, Parent teacher meetings putting them in dance classes and all holidays, but the scale still tilted to where it appeared I was always absent. For me I was in survival mode. I knew I had to bring money into the household; The pressure was real; Wayne was the provider and protector in my life but now I was navigating life without him. I would quietly give my mother money to make the burden a little lighter for taking care of my 2 daughters. There were moments when she would stop me from going out and tell me take your children home, they need to be in their own beds and I need a break, It wasn't just my children by this time my sister had her children they were known as the Stairsteps because we had them one after another. The blessing is they are still close today; her words she drilled into me and my siblings all the time was "Stick Together" was now being reinforced with me and my sisters' children. Dee Dee was an amazing mother grandmother and woman. I was a public star in the community, a self-made success pushing myself onto every prestigious stage, but I felt like a failure in my own home. I never once heard my children express pride or excitement about my music career; instead, I felt a quiet, persistent detachment. I know they deserved more from me, but I was constantly struggling to bridge the gap created by my own unresolved grief.

The Rift and the Rebuilding the Rift I created manifested as a profound emotional distance. I saw the reflections of my own "Running" years mirrored in my children's eyes, and the silence between us became a language of its own. As a mother, I had to learn to honor the walls they built for their own protection. But I thank God that those walls are coming down. I know that anything that has been broken down can be rebuilt—one brick at a time. One "Love Brick" at a time. Through Christ, all things are possible, and what I have learned is that Love Never Fails. Love speaks to the heart; Love speaks to the mind; Love rebuilds; and most importantly, Love stays.

COUNSELOR'S INSIGHT:

THE ARCHITECTURE OF REBUILDING

When a relationship has been "Stained" by years of absence or silence, our first instinct is to want a "Quick Fix." We want to tear the whole wall down in a single day.

But true Restoration is architectural—it is a slow, sacred process of reconstruction. You cannot force a heart to open; you can only provide the safety for it to bloom.

The Three Pillars of the "Love Brick" Strategy:

- **Patience:** Waiting for the "emotional cement" to dry before trying to add more weight.
- **Precision:** Placing one "Love Brick" (a sincere apology, a consistent phone call, a shared meal) with intentionality.
- **Presence:** Refusing to run when the conversation gets heavy or the silence gets loud.

YOUR TURN TO BREATHE

Reflecting on the "Love Bricks" Restoration is not a sprint; it is a steady walk toward the heart of another. It requires laying down our "Right to be Right" in exchange for the "Grace to be Present." In the space below, identify one "Love Brick" you can offer a loved one today to begin rebuilding a bridge that has been damaged by the silence of the past.

My Love Brick for today is:

____

____

____

____

____

____

____

____

____

THE HEARTS WITHOUT WALLS PRAYER

Lord, we lift every family dynamic that has been fractured by the "Running" years. We pray for the mothers who carry the weight of "What I should have done" and the children who carry the weight of "What wasn't there."

We thank You that You are the Master Builder. Give us the grace to lay down our guilt and pick up a "Love Brick." We declare that no silence is too deep for Your voice to reach, and no wall is too high for Your love to climb. We trust You with the rebuilding of our homes. In Jesus' Name, Amen.

Chapter 6: The Nail in the Emotional Coffin

At this time, I was dating a man I'll call BB. He was one of the best relationships I had because of his genuine care for me, though he was someone who carried many stains in his own life. This triple blow— my anchor my mother gone, a new life to manage alone my youngest daughter, and the betrayal of yet another relationship—was the perfect storm that led to my final collapse. BB immediately said no to my request to travel. "Sunshine, I really don't want you involved in my dealings," he insisted. "I always want to protect you." After begging him, he finally gave in. I knew the trip was dangerous, but I needed to escape the guilt and the silence of my home more than I needed safety. Before we left, I made one desperate attempt for comfort and safety. I reached out to the one person I needed most, asking for a place to simply rest for the night to gather myself. That comfort was not available to me. In that moment of utter vulnerability, the feeling of total rejection slammed shut the last door of hope. That was the nail in my emotional coffin. At that point, I truly didn't care what happened; I just needed to get away.

We left, and I felt okay about leaving my two-year-old with her Godmother. We were driving on the New Jersey Turnpike when the flashing lights appeared in the rearview mirror. We were stopped by a state trooper, and we were all arrested.

I remember sitting on the cold pavement in the dead of winter, freezing, as they picked me up and handcuffed me. We were taken to a small-town courthouse and given a substantial bail of twenty-five thousand dollars.

New York Class

"After my mother passed, the silence was deafening. She had been my anchor, the one person I could bounce my world off and without her, the darkness of a deep depression began to cave in. I wasn't just traveling; I was running because the voices in my head had become too loud to bear. As I reached for the car door to start that trip, I heard a still, small voice that suddenly felt like it was shouting through a bullhorn inside my soul: 'Do not get in the car. Do not go.' But the weight of my depression overlapped the warning. I ignored the bullhorn, stepped into the car, and headed straight toward the 'Nail in the Coffin' waiting for me on the New Jersey Turnpike." I was taken to the female jail. I could see the tears in BB's eyes as they took me away, but I was numb—I had been numb for a long time. It was the weekend, and nothing moved in the courts on the weekend.

When I woke up the next morning, I was violently sick. My fever was very high, and what happened next was a signal that God saw me and helped me. He used a group of women who immediately recognized, from the looks of me, that I didn't belong in there. This group of women took care of me, kept me warm, and consoled and protected me. They started calling me New York Class "They soon found out I was a singer and would ask me to sing, but I was too broken to bring a single note of music from my mouth. As I looked around that dingy, dirty jail where hundreds of women were held, I was thinking every minute of the day: *'How did I get here?'*

My thoughts spiraled. Now I was going to have a criminal record. I had let my desperation push me over a huge cliff. I called my youngest daughter's godmother and begged her, **'Please, don't tell anyone.'** My mother—my only natural help in a time of trouble—was gone. I knew the news would spread like wildfire in the streets of Harlem, and I wasn't going to ask for help. I was in the trench."

The Voice in the Trench

Each day, I prayed for God to help me or tell me who to call. By day six, I could feel a trench of despair coming over me. I closed my eyes, and I distinctly heard my mother's voice: "Stop crying, Sheila, and do something. Get it together!"

Then, I thought of my dear special friend, Barbara. I walked to the phone and called her. She couldn't believe what I was telling her, but she simply said, "I will be to see you soon."

I learned how to live in those circumstances. I was told, "Never leave your cup unattended, always watch over your soap and your utensils because as quick as you turn your head, your things will be gone." Three weeks passed. Barbara kept her word and came to see me. My bail was still twenty-five thousand dollars. BB was still trying relentlessly to reach the judge on my behalf, explaining I was innocent and didn't know he had drugs in the car.

One day, they called my name and said it was time for my court date. I was a mess, trying to stay calm. As I stood in front of the judge, he wanted to know how I got myself mixed up with a criminal like BB. They knew I had no arrest record, and the attorney shared that I was a professional singer. The judge lowered my bail to ten percent of the ten thousand. I called Barbara, and she paid it for me. When I was released, I ran to see my youngest daughter; I missed her so much. Somehow, she had become my lifeline since my mother passed. There were many nights while carrying her I would pull strength from her. She was two years old now and I was so excited to run to her.

One evening, I was at a friend's house and received a phone call from a childhood friend. She asked me to go to church with her.

This was the turning point of my life. The Stain would have to face a power greater than my pain. I accepted her invitation, and on this cold February morning, I met the Lord and had an encounter with him. My life has never been the same.

Counselor's Insight: The Divine Collision

In my counseling room, I often tell people that "Rock Bottom" is a solid foundation if you find the Lord there. For decades, I tried to manage the **Stain** with my voice, my career, and my "Great Escapes." But on that cold February morning, I finally ran out of places to hide.

When the "Power greater than my pain" stepped into that space, the **Stain** didn't just fade—it met its Master. We often fear the "Unraveling" because we think we are falling apart, but God is pulling the threads of our old life so He can weave a garment of **Kabod** (Glory).

"I was naked, and ye clothed me: I was sick, and ye visited me: I was in prison, and ye came unto me." — **Matthew 25:3**

The K-A-B-O-D Reflection

The Weight of the Encounter

- *Can you name the "February Morning" in your own life—the moment when your power ran out and God's power began?*
- *If you are currently in the middle of an "Unraveling," can you trust that it is actually a setup for a Divine Collision?*

A Moment in the Kabod Room:

The Mercy of the Trench

Pastor Sheila's Reflection: "I spent 1986 running as fast as I could, but it all ended on the frozen ground of a January night. By the time I reached the jail cell, I was violently sick, stripped of my coat and my pride. But God's Grace had already gone before me. He placed women in that cell who didn't know my name or my 'Gilded Escape,' yet they nursed me back to health. They saw a need that I couldn't even voice. I had to learn how to just *be*—to be the one who was cared for instead of the one always taking care of others. It was my first lesson in true 'Kabod'—that His glory often wears the face of the people the world has discarded, reaching out to you when you're at your lowest."

Your Turn to Breathe: *Who are the 'Nameless Angels' God has placed in your path during your darkest moments?*

- **The Exposure:** What 'protection' has been taken away from you lately, leaving you feeling exposed to the cold?

- **The Vulnerability:** Is it hard for you to stop being the 'Rock' and let someone else care for you? Why do we feel we have to stay strong even when we are breaking?

- **The Mercy:** Can you see 'Grace' in your current struggle? Even in a place of consequence, where is the mercy that is nursing you back to life?

Counselor's Insight: The Divine Collision

in Chapter 6, I describe the moment I accepted the invitation to face power greater than my pain. In my practice, I call this a "Divine Collision." We spend our lives trying to avoid the "trench," but sometimes God allows us to hit the bottom so we can finally stop running and start resting. A collision with Grace doesn't break you; it breaks the *stain* off you. It is the end of the "Gilded Escape" and the beginning of the "Kabod Restoration."

The Kabod Reflection: The Mercy of the Trench
That cold February morning wasn't just a religious moment; it was a life-saving encounter. I was in a trench of depression, but I found mercy there.

- **Your Turn to Breathe:** Have you ever felt like you were in a "trench" so deep you couldn't see the light? What if that trench isn't your burial ground, but the very place where God is waiting to collide with your heart? Name one thing you are ready to surrender in your "Divine Collision" today.

Hearts Without Walls Bridge A "Divine Collision" changes the way you breathe. You no longer have to gasp for air in the "Neon Lights"; you can finally inhale the peace of the Father. At **Hearts Without Walls**, we believe that once you meet the Lord in the trench, you never have to walk alone again. If you are ready for your life to never be the same, take a deep breath. This is your **Oxygen**.

The Oxygen: A Heart Without Walls Prayer "Lord God, thank You for this day. Order my steps in the way I shall go. Thank You for Your continuous provision and comfort that You give me in my time of suffering. May I feel Your healing touch; restore my body and rejuvenate my mind, especially when I feel discouraged. You give me such confidence in the power of Your grace that even when I am afraid, I know I must put on my whole armor of God. Lord, I will trust You and I will pray to You. I will believe You and continue to stand on Your Word. I love You. In Jesus' name I pray. Amen."

Counselor's Insight: The Bowing of the Stain

In my counseling practice, we talk about **"Reframing."** When I was 17, the **Stain** was my master; it told me who I was and where I could go. But through the **Spiritual Intervention** of Chapter 7, the hierarchy changed.

When you encounter the transformative power of grace, your struggles don't just disappear, they become your **credentials**. The very things that once "held me back" became the "proof" that God can fix what is broken. The environment around you may still feel "dim" (like a prison cell or a lonely house), but your internal light has been switched on.

The K-A-B-O-D Reflection

The Weight of Grace:

- **Reflect:** What "Struggle" in your life is currently trying to "hold you back"? What would happen if you forced that struggle to "bow" to the Love of God today?
- **Identify:** Can you see your "Stains" as future "Proof" of God's power, rather than permanent marks of your failure?

Chapter 7: The Pivot

Be still, and know that I am God" Psalm 46:10

The jail cell, the cold pavement, and the fear of a criminal record and facing a jail sentence had been the final, brutal act of the Stain. The Gilded Escape had failed utterly, leaving me broken and exposed. But in that complete brokenness, a new path was cleared. When I was released on bail, the shame was a heavy cloak. I ran straight to see my two-year-old, my youngest daughter, whom I had missed desperately. But the memory of the rejection right before my arrest—when I had begged someone close to me to give me refuge, they told me NO—this was the final hammer blow. The cost was immeasurable. I was back in Harlem, but I was not back in my life. I was a ghost, waiting for the legal system to define my future. The music felt dead, and the silence in my soul was deafening.

One evening, while at a friend's house, I got a phone call from a friend I grew up with. She asked me a simple question that became the pivot point of my entire existence: "Will you go to church with me?"

The Cold February Morning and the Divine Collision
The cold pavement of the New Jersey jail and the stale smoke of the after-hours clubs were still fresh in my memory, and yet, here was an invitation to something clean, something lasting. The Stain, which thrives in darkness, had to now face a direct light.

I accepted her invitation.

On that cold February morning, I walked into the sanctuary. The atmosphere was a profound contrast to the chaos I had just left. As I entered, the powerful sound of a Hammond B3 organ filled the air, backed by the sharp beat of drums and the rhythmic clapping of hands. This was a Pentecostal church The Bible Church of Christ, Bronx New York, a stark difference from the quiet Baptist Temple church my mother used to take us to in Harlem. I followed my friend inside, and though she wanted to be close to the front, we sat in the middle of the congregation where I felt a little less exposed under the gaze of what felt like hundreds of people. For the first time since Wayne's death, the noise in my mind was not louder than the environment I was in. I felt a sudden, profound calm—a stillness that was terrifyingly new.

The preacher found his scripture and began to speak about God's love and the promise of change. I was listening intently, deeply depressed, still wrestling with the crushing grief of my mother's recent death and the abandonment by the father of my youngest daughter. My mind spiraled back to the humiliation of the jail cell, and tears flooded my eyes. I prayed silently in my spirit, sinking into a trance of despair.

My friend touched me, breaking the trance: "They are calling for prayer. Would you like to go up?"

I hesitated, feeling the eyes of the huge congregation, but her assurance—"I will go with you"—felt like a lifeline. Walking toward the altar felt like moving in slow motion. I waited until an Elder reached her hand out. She asked what I needed prayer for, and as I began to tell her the tangle of my heart—the losses, the guilt, the abandonments, she stopped me gently. "Lift your hands," she instructed.

As she began to pray, a powerful, physical sensation took hold. I felt someone leave me followed by a distinct sound, like air being let out of a tire. I found myself collapsing in front of the altar, crying out, "Thank you, Jesus!" I then heard my own voice speaking in other tongues—a language I didn't know, a spontaneous, uncontrollable release that my natural mind couldn't rationalize. My friends were around me, one who is now a Prophetess who would constantly tell me and my siblings that her and her husband had been constantly praying for us. My dear friend who extended the invitation to get me in the house of the Lord was overjoyed. The Joy on their faces as they all led me back to my seat, was priceless. I was feeling as if a High Riser building had been released off my shoulders. In that encounter, I knew God was real and loved me. He had rescued me, delivering me from the desire for any substance, and erasing loneliness. The empty hole in me, I realized, was designed for the Lord to fill. My entire life changed on that cold February day in the Bronx. I was now free to learn how to start over without the Stain yelling at me, without the Stain robbing me again. My experience was an encounter with the Father—He rescued and delivered me. I know that everyone's experience with God is different, but mine was a direct intervention a collision. My intensity now was not running away but rushing to Him in worship and devotion.

I began to grapple with the deepest, most complex act of forgiveness: I had to forgive Wayne for leaving, and I had to stop tying myself in knots trying to understand and blame myself for his death. This was the final chain the Stain had on me. Forgiveness looked like letting go of the question, Why ? did he walk into that tailor shop and never walk out?

It was in this light that I realized a profound truth: My Impediment is my testimony. The very struggles and stains that had held me back were now proof of the transformative power of grace. I was on my way to a brighter day and future, even though the environment around me felt dim. My life has never been the same. The Stain would have to bow to the power of love that can never be separated.

"Who shall separate us from the love of Christ? Shall trouble or hardship or persecution or famine or nakedness or danger or sword? ... No, in all these things we are more than conquerors through him who loved us." — Romans 8:35, 37

A Moment in the Kabod Room

The Pivot

Pastor Sheila's Reflection:

"I walked into that Bronx church carrying the heavy silence of my mother's absence. She had been my anchor, and without her, I felt like I was drifting in a deep, dark depression. But at that altar, the 'Gilded Escape' finally stopped. I didn't find a religion; I found a **Presence**.

Every layer of being downtrodden, every shadow of the 'Stain,' and every ounce of grief was suddenly and violently lifted. I stood up from that altar feeling a relief I hadn't never known before. I wasn't a 'Runner' anymore; I was a daughter who had finally found her true home."

Your Turn to Breathe: *Have you ever reached a point where 'trying' to be okay wasn't enough, and you just needed a Heavenly Encounter?*

- **The Lifting:** If you could feel total relief from one thing today—just like I felt at that altar—what would it be?

- **The New Anchor:** When the person you relied on most is gone, who is the one 'Presence' that can fill that void for you?

- **Freedom:** What does 'Freedom' look like to you? Is it a feeling, a place, or a person?

The Scriptural Anchor:

"Now the Lord is that Spirit: and where the Spirit of the Lord is, there is liberty." — ***2 Corinthians 3:17***

Counselor's Insight: The Spiritual Intervention (The Pivot) In Chapter 7, we explore the "Spiritual Intervention" that forces a life to pivot. In my counseling practice, I often see people trying to "manage" their pain, but management is not a miracle. A pivot happens when you realize that your stain cannot coexist with the glory of God's love. One of them must bow. When you decide that the "Fading Stain" no longer has the final say, you create space for a miracle to be performed in the very place where you were once broken.

The Kabod Reflection: The Power of the Bow My life has never been the same since that intervention; I realized that God's love is a force that cannot be separated from me.

- **Breathe:** What is the "stain" in your life that you have been allowing to sit on the throne? Are you ready to command it to bow to the power of a Love that will never leave you nor forsake you? If you could name one miracle God has performed in your "Pivot," what would it be?

The Hearts Without Walls Bridge A pivot is the moment you stop looking back at what broke you and start looking up at the One who is building you. At **Hearts Without Walls**, we believe that gratitude is the fuel for your new direction. If you are ready to walk away from the stain and into the wonders of His faithfulness, take a deep breath. This is your **Oxygen**.

The Oxygen: A Heart Without Walls Prayer "Lord Jesus, thank You for another day. It is Your name that is above every name. Thank You for always being faithful; thank You for never leaving me nor forsaking me. Father, thank You for Your unconditional love. I thank You for all the wonders You have worked and the miracles You have performed. Thank You, Lord, for the peace that passes all understanding. In Jesus' Name I Pray, Amen."

THE DIVINE COLLISION

Scripture Anchor: *"Who shall separate us from the love of Christ? Shall tribulation, or distress, or persecution, or famine, or nakedness, or peril, or sword?"* —

Romans 8:35

COUNSELOR'S INSIGHT: THE PHYSIOLOGY OF SURRENDER

As a Licensed Professional Counselor, I look back at that altar in the Bronx and see more than just a spiritual moment; I see a **neurological reset**. Trauma lives in the body. It lives in the "high-rise building" of tension on your shoulders and the "tire-pressure" of anxiety in your chest.

When you truly surrender, your nervous system finally exits "Fight or Flight" mode. For the first time in years, your brain can process grief without being overwhelmed by it. Surrender isn't "giving up"—it is reclaiming your right to breathe. It is the moment you stop managing the "Stain" and start allowing Grace to dissolve it.

YOUR TURN TO BREATHE: EXHALING THE WEIGHT

Sheila felt the "air let out of the tire" and a "building lifted off her shoulders." Recovery often starts with a physical release. In the space below, identify the "Weight" you have been carrying for too long.

What is the "High-Rise Building" on your shoulders today?

What would your life look like if you finally let that "Air out of the tire"?

PASTOR SHEILA'S REFLECTION: THE FINAL CHAIN

The most difficult part of my "Collision" wasn't the tongues or the crying—it was the forgiveness. I had to forgive a ghost. I had to let go of the "Why" regarding Wayne's death.

If you are waiting for an explanation before you forgive, you will be a prisoner forever. Forgiveness is not about the other person's actions; it is about your own Liberty. Today, I declare that the "Final Chain" is broken over your life. You don't need to understand the "Why" to receive the "Now."

THE "RECLAMATION" PRAYER

Lord, we thank You for the Divine Collision. We thank You that You meet us in our deepest depression and our darkest cells. I pray for the one reading this who feels like a 'Ghost' in their own life. Let them feel the 'Air' being let out of their trauma right now. Lift the building off their shoulders. Replace their 'Why' with Your 'Will.' In the Matchless Name of Jesus, Amen.

**The Unraveling had stopped, and the reconstruction had begun. **

Chapter 8: The Reconstruction

The Erased Record

"I, even I, am he who blots out your transgressions for my own sake and remembers your sins no more".

The physical feeling of the "High Riser building" being lifted from my shoulders was the first sign that the Stain was in retreat. The spiritual encounter at the altar had broken its hold, but the real work—the Reconstruction—was just beginning. I had to learn how to live in the quiet space I had finally earned.

I embraced the scripture:

"Therefore, if anyone is in Christ, he is a new creation: the old has passed away; behold, all things have become new." — 2 Corinthians 5:17

This was my blueprint. The old life of chaotic performances, smoky after-hours clubs, and running on adrenaline was over. I had been given a new spirit, and I had to rebuild my habits to match it.

The New Sound of Silence

The hardest part of the early weeks was the quiet. For years, the silence of my grief had been chased away by the thunderous applause of the crowd, the bass of the nightclub, or the anxiety of the hustle. Now, I chose to sit in the quiet. I traded my tailored gowns for casual clothes and my microphone for my Bible. My first act of reconstruction was finding stillness and learning how to pray again, not just in silent desperation, but in daily devotion.

I am a practical person, and my transformation was internal—not a radical external cleansing. I didn't need to throw out my old contact lists or records; music is universal, and my change was of the heart. The desire to engage in the chaotic life of the after-hours scene was simply gone. I began a new walk, and I never slipped back into those old ways because the new direction was firm. The old life centered on the Gilded Escape was over, not because I destroyed the artifacts of my career, but because the spirit that drove me to perform was now driving me to serve. The change in my heart made my Harlem neighborhood, which had once felt like home, now feel different— no longer a stage for performance, but a place for service. The guilt that once drove me to hide now compelled me to seek light.

IT NEVER HAPPENED! (The Legal Miracle)

The immediate, crippling anxiety was the criminal charge hanging over my head. I had been released on bail, but the court date and the possibility of a permanent criminal record and serving a sentence felt like the final, physical mark the Stain would leave.

It was a sunny day in my Harlem apartment, and the phone rang. It was BB. He had been calling me each day to check on me, so happy that I was back home. His voice was pleasant and sweet as usual.

"Sunshine, I have some good news for you," he said.

I braced myself, thinking he was about to share that he was coming home. Instead, he told me the State Trooper who pulled us over and made the arrests was in the paper for corruption. He was being investigated and charged for stealing evidence and general wrongdoing.

I couldn't believe it. BB and I were screaming and laughing and thanking God. He explained that every case the corrupt State Trooper had touched would be thrown out of court, including mine, because the evidence was tainted and the arrests were questionable.

I had no record. In other words, IT NEVER HAPPENED!

The Stain had tried to mark me with a legal consequence, something that would stop me from getting a job, from traveling, from ever truly feeling free. And in one sovereign, miraculous act, God reached down and erased it completely, making the past charge legally void. I could not deny that this was the definitive confirmation that my encounter at the altar was real.

I was still very concerned about BB, but he asked me to go on with my life, explaining that he would be continuing to serve an old sentence from a prior case. I felt a deep loyalty to him for his genuine care and kindness, and I refused to accept that he was "not good enough."

"Maybe not on paper," I told him, "But in your heart, you are good enough for me."

But he insisted, protecting me even from behind bars. Eventually, BB was sent upstate to finish his sentence, now with another charge on him, and I never saw him again until some twenty-five years later at a funeral. Our eyes locked, and I felt something in my heart as our unspoken words spoke silently to each other. He was the final, complicated tie to my past life of running, and it was a clean break, blessed by God.

The New Anointing and Service

With the emotional and legal Stain removed, I immediately joined the music ministry at the church where I was attending. My voice—the one that had belted out disco and jazz to a crowd of gilded escapists—is finally being used for its true purpose. The singing that had once been my chaotic mask is now a pure offering of worship.

This time, the energy I poured into my calling was not to escape, but to anchor myself to something real. I went back to school for my counseling degree prioritizing informal wisdom I had dispensed in those smoky after-hours clubs into a true profession of service.

I was now equipped to truly help people suffering the same despair that had nearly consumed me. I began to record Gospel music and was booked nationally and internationally as a singer and minister, teaching the word of God. I was then ordained as a Pastor, serving the people of God. The Stain has tried to recur in my walk with the Lord, but the difference is, I am not alone. I know who I am and the plans He has for me.

The journey taught me that my freedom came not through human effort, but through divine grace:

"Now the Lord is the Spirit, and where the Spirit of the Lord is, there is liberty." — 2 Corinthians 3:17

The bondage of the Stain—the guilt, the fear, the desire to run—has bowed by God's power and love.

I have once again mentioned that I have returned to ask for forgiveness from my children, and I have done my part. I am free. Truly, when we stop running and surrender to the one who said we are fearfully and wonderfully made, He reminds us that He knitted us in our mother's womb and that He called us from the foundation of the earth. The Unraveling had stopped, and the reconstruction was a success.

A Moment in the Kabod Room:

(The Divine Eraser)

Pastor Sheila's Reflection:

"I spent my life trying to outrun the 'Stains' of my past, only to find myself in a jail cell in 1986. I was terrified that a criminal record would be the final, permanent mark on my name. But then came the phone call: the state trooper was a 'dirty cop,' and the case was dismissed. It was as if God had taken His hand and swiped it across the chalkboard of my life. The world said I was a 'Runner,' but God said, **'It never happened.'** He didn't just forgive me; He vindicated me. He took the 'Nail in the Coffin' and used it to nail my past to the Cross once and for all."

Your Turn to Breathe: *What 'record' have you been carrying in your mind that God has already cleared?*

- **The Eraser:** If God told you today that the one thing you are most ashamed of 'never happened' in His eyes, how would you walk differently?

- **The Vindicated Heart:** Who or what has been trying to hold your past against you? Can you choose to listen to 'Good News' instead of Old Charges'?

- **The New Name:** Now that the record is clear, what 'New Name' is God giving you? (Is it Counselor? Pastor? Restorer?)

The Scriptural Anchor:

"As far as the east is from the west, so far hath he removed our transgressions from us." — ***Psalm 103:12***

Dear Lord, today put pressure on my problem, take the weight off what worries me. Lord speak loudly so I can be silent and breakdown every barrier blocking my breakthrough Lord bring joy and peace to my family and encouragement to our childrenand strength to my body in Jesus' name I pray. Amen

Chapter 9: The Faded Stain

Conclusion

"Go ye into all the world, and preach the gospel to every creature"- Mark 16:15

The Stain came into three parts: the **Inherited Burden** of my childhood, the **Immediate Crush** of my teenage loss, and the **Self-Imposed Consequence** of my chaotic escape. It dictated my identity for decades, turning me into a runner, a people-pleaser, and a woman who sought control in every environment except her own heart.

But as I stand here today, an ordained Pastor and a woman walking in the liberty of Christ, I can testify that the Stain has faded. It is not erased—scars rarely disappear entirely—but the destructive power it once held over my mind, body, and soul is broken. Surrender, Not Struggle. I spent my youth trying to be the Peacemaker, the girl who could fix her father's rage, and the star who could distract herself from her husband's grave. When I heard my mother declare, "You are now Sheila, you are a woman," the burden of being perfect was officially placed on my shoulders. I carried that burden everywhere, until it finally collapsed on me in a jail cell. The final lesson of the Stain is this: it is never defeated by fighting, but by surrender.

My spiritual intervention and the subsequent miracle of the erased criminal charge taught me that I did not have to earn my freedom. My freedom was paid for by grace. It was the Lord's power that ensured the old passed away and that all things truly became new.

My life became a testament to 2 Corinthians 4:8-9: "We are hard pressed on every side but not crushed; perplexed, but not in despair; persecuted but not abandoned; struck down but not destroyed."

I have been hard-pressed many times, but I was never crushed. My children and I were struck down by the tragedy of Wayne's death and my subsequent running, but we were not destroyed. For His strength has made me strong, and His support has kept me anchored to the Vine.

The Final Act of Forgiveness

The deepest part of my healing was not found in the pulpit or on a stage; it was found in the painful silence of acceptance with my daughters.

I have asked for their forgiveness, and they have granted it. Yet, the spiritual maturity I have gained has taught me that the deepest forgiveness is the one I must give to myself, and the deepest love is the one I must practice without condition.

I had to stop expecting. I had to let go of the fight to be the perfect mother, the perfect widow, the perfect woman, and simply accept the reality of our shared pain. I lay down the emotional fight, and I have learned to love them where they are, wanting nothing but the best for them.

When I stopped fighting for their approval, I finally became free. This is the truth of Biblical Forgiveness:

releasing resentment and the desire to make the offender pay.

The journey through the Inherited Stain and the Immediate Stain has taught my daughters and me the same ultimate truth: "It's not how you start; it's how you finish." The chaos, the trauma, the music, the jail cell—all of it was simply the process. The finish is here, in the liberty of the Holy Spirit.

The Stain has faded from my mind, body, and soul. And the Blood still speaks:

> *"to Jesus, the mediator of a new covenant, and to the sprinkled blood that speaks a better word than the blood of Abel."* — **Hebrews 12:24**

The Blood of Abel cried out for vengeance; Jesus' blood, in contrast, speaks of forgiveness, mercy, and reconciliation.

ONE DAY IN MY QUIET TIME THE LORD DOWNLOADED THESE LYRICS TO ME, I CALLED A PRODUCER FRIEND OF MINE WE WORKED TO GET A BEAUTIFUL MELODY.

TO MY READER, I WANT YOU TO KNOW "THE BLOOD STILL SPEAKS"

LYRICS: THE BLOOD STILL SPEAKS

WRITTEN & SUNG BY: SHEILA INGRAM

ON ALL DIGITAL OUTLES; APPLE, SPOTIFY

****

VERSE; IN THE HUSH OF THE MORING

AS THE SUN PEEKS THROUGH

YOUR VOICE REMINDS ME ITS ALL BRAND NEW

THE WEIGHT OF THE WORLD MAY TRY
TO PULL ME DOWN BUT YOUR LOVE
SURROUNDS ME WITH A CONSTANT
JOYFUL SOUND

OH, YOUR BLOOD STILL SPEAKS

OF CHAINS UNDONE AND SPIRITS
HIGH

SALVATION SONG RINGS FULL AND
FREE

YOUR BLOOD STILL SPEAKS OF VICTORY

THAT'S WHY I COME INTO YOUR
PRESENCE

I WILL BOW BEFORE YOUR THRONE

OHHH JESUS

2X THE BLOOD STILL SPEAKS; YOUR
BLOOD STILL SPEAKS OH LORD-----------

MMMM …YOUR BLOOD STILL SPEAKS,
MY LORD

CHOURUS.

IT SPEAKS OF GRACE

IT SPEAKS OF FREEDOM

IT SPEAKS OF LOVE

THE BLOOD STILL SPEAKS

ANSWERS TO THE SINNERS CRY

2X JESUS SAID YOUR CAINS ARE BROKEN

JUST COME ALIVE, COME ALIVE

THERES POWER IN THE BLOOD, HALLELEUAH

CHORUS, MUSIC, OUT

Epilogue: The Liberty of the Holy Spirit

The journey from a seventeen-year-old widow to an ordained Pastor was not a straight line; it was a devastating detour dictated by a trauma I spent decades trying to control. I started this memoir by detailing the three parts of The Stain—The Inherited Burden, The Immediate Crush, and The Self-Imposed Consequence—and I end it with the testimony of a woman set free.

If you have walked with me through these pages, you know that my freedom did not come from willpower, success, or human effort. It came through total collapse and divine intervention. It came when I realized that the silence in my soul was not the absence of sound, but the absence of God.

The greatest lesson I carried out of the jail cell and into my new life was this: You cannot earn what is freely given. I spent my youth trying to earn worth, earn love, and earn forgiveness. The Lord showed me that my worth was intrinsic, my love was unearned, and my forgiveness was paid for long before I ever sinned. The physical miracle of my criminal charge being erased legally voided the Stain's claim over my future.

Today, my life is a monument to the simple truth found in the Word of God:

"Now the Lord is the Spirit, and where the Spirit of the Lord is, there is liberty." — 2 Corinthians 3:17

Liberty is not just freedom from a jail sentence; it is freedom from the relentless cycle of guilt, self-blame, and running. It is the peace of acceptance, especially regarding the deep, complex love I share with my daughters. I honor their distance and cherish their presence, knowing that my role is to stand in the freedom I have found and continue to pray for their own healing.

The Stain on my soul has not been wiped clean by a cloth but washed away by the blood of mercy.

Whatever your own Stain may be—a loss, a failure, a chaotic choice—I want you to know that the Lord is the ultimate reconstructor. He takes the wreckage of our worst choices and builds a foundation of grace.

In my clinical practice, we often talk about **"Deconstruction"**—breaking down the old, faulty beliefs we've carried about our worth. But without **Reconstruction**, we are just left with a pile of rubble. Chapter 8 is the proof that God doesn't just stop the "Unraveling" of our lives; He begins a Master Build.

When you finally stop running and surrender, you allow the Original Architect to remind you of your **Foundational Identity.** You weren't a "mistake" in Harlem; you were **knitted** with intention. You weren't a "failure" as a young widow; you were **called** from the foundation of the earth. The reconstruction is a success not because the pain never happened, but because the **Anchor** is finally in the right place.

The K-A-B-O-D Reflection (The Weight of Identity):

- **Reflect:** If you stopped "Reconstructing" yourself based on your past failures and let God "Reconstruct" you based on His Word (Psalm 139), what would change about your tomorrow?

- **Action:** Read Psalm 139:13-16 aloud. Which part of being "fearfully and wonderfully made" is the hardest for you to believe about yourself today? That is the area where the Reconstruction is currently working.

Your Turn to Breathe: *What 'wreckage' in your life are you currently staring at? Is it a broken relationship, a career setback, or a personal failure?*

- **The Blueprints:** If God is the Architect of your life, what new 'room' is He building in you right now? (Is it a room of Peace? Wisdom? Strength?)

- **The Foundation:** Is your life built on the 'Stain' of what happened to you, or the 'Grace' of what God has done for you?

- **The Tools:** What is one 'tool' of grace you can use today to start rebuilding your joy? (Is it prayer, counseling, or simply being still?)

The Scriptural Anchor

*"For I know the thoughts that I think toward you, saith the Lord, thoughts of peace, and not of evil, to give you an expected end." — **Jeremiah 29:11***

Counselor's Insight: The Ultimate Constructor in Chapter 9, I share that whatever your "stain" may be—a failure, a chaotic choice, or a secret shame—the Lord is the Ultimate Constructor. In my counseling practice, I often see people trying to hide their "wreckage" under the rug. But a good builder knows you can't build on top of debris. You must let the Lord sort through the wreckage of your worst choices. He doesn't throw away the broken pieces; He reinforces them with His strength until they become the most solid part of your foundation.

The Hearts Without Walls Bridge A "Foundation of Grace" is the only thing strong enough to hold up a Heart Without Walls. When the wreckage is in His hands, the pressure is off of you. At **Hearts Without Walls,** we believe that your worst choice doesn't have to be your last word. If you are ready to stop hiding the rubble and start building the restoration, take a deep breath. This is your **Oxygen**.

Oxygen: A Heart Without Walls Prayer "Good morning, Father. Please send an abundance of faith, peace, and calm to our family, friends, and colleagues. I want them to know that You have heard our prayers and have seen all tears, and You will answer our prayers according to the will for our lives. Lord, it is because of You we move, breathe, and have our being. Thank You for forgiveness. In Jesus' Name I Pray,

Chapter 10 (The Professional Pivot)

Pastor Sheila's Reflection:

"People often ask me why I needed a license when I already had the Holy Spirit. My answer is always the same: **God uses the natural to manifest the supernatural.** My education gave me the tools to bridge the gap between the 'Pulpit' and the 'Pavement.' I realized that the 17-year-old widow didn't just need a prayer; she needed a plan. The 'Stain' taught me how to feel; my credentials taught me how to heal. I am a witness that it is never too late to pick up a new mantle."

- **Education:** What is one thing you've always wanted to learn that could help you serve others better?
- **The Bridge:** How can you use your professional life (your job, your skills) to be a bridge for God's Grace?

- **The New Chapter:** If age is just a number and Grace is the fuel, what is the next big 'Yes' you need to say to God

The Scriptural Anchor:

"Study to shew thyself approved unto God, a workman that needeth not to be ashamed, rightly dividing the word of truth."
— 2 Timothy 2:15

Counselor's Insight: The Professional Pivot (The Integrated Life) In Chapter 10, I addressed the question I often hear: "Why do you need a license when you have the Holy Spirit?" In my counseling practice, I call this **"Integrated Life."** The Holy Spirit is our Comforter and Guide, but God also gave us the gift of wisdom and specialized training to heal the mind. A pivot happens when you stop separating your "sacred" life from your "secular" career. When you bring the Kabod into the counseling room or the boardroom, you aren't just doing a job, you are fulfilling a mandate.

The Kabod Reflection: The Weight of Your Mandate My license is a tool, but the Holy Spirit is the Power. Together, they create a space for deep restoration that moves beyond the surface.

- **Your Turn to Breathe:** In what area of your professional life have you been keeping the Holy Spirit "at the door"? If you were to pivot today and see your career as a ministry, how would that change the way you treat your clients, colleagues, or customers? Name one professional goal you are ready to surrender to His purpose.

The Hearts Without Walls Bridge A Heart Without Walls doesn't have "office hours." It is open and available to be used by God anywhere—from the pulpit to the therapy couch. At **Hearts Without Walls**, we believe that your professional pivot is just another way for the Father to order your steps. If you are ready to see your career as your "Kabod Room," take a deep breath. This is your **Oxygen**.

The Oxygen: A Heart Without Walls Prayer "Father God, I trust that You are in Control. Regulate my mind Father, I shall not give attention to the spirit of fear and anxiety. Surround me with Your peace that surpasses all understanding. Raise me up in Your victorious right hand. Walk with me through challenges that have presented themselves. Grant me Your strength. Help me, God, to focus on You and not on my problems. I know that You, God, are bigger than all of it.

Thank You for strength, that I may soar on wings like eagles. In Jesus' Name I Pray, Amen."

The Hall of Faith:
Sister-to-Sister

THE RAHAB REDEMPTION ...Joshua sent spies to Jericho, and they lodged at the house of Rahab, the prostitute. Her quick thinking gave them time and opportunity to get back to their camp. In return, she asked that they spare her family from death. The spies guaranteed safety if her family remained in her home during the onslaught and scarlet rope was in her window. When the city of Jericho was being taken, Rahab and her family were rescued and led out to place outside of the camp. Rahab later became the wife of Salmon, the great-great-grandmother of King David, and an ancestor of

Jesus Christ. Believers can glean from Rahab's life as she was a woman of faith, courage, and love.

Your past was a dress rehearsal for your future!!!

You Qualify! You Paid a Price. Never be around people who tolerate you Pivot and be around people who celebrate you.

Know your worth!!!!

The Rahab Redemption: It's Not How You Start; It's How You Finish

"By faith the harlot Rahab perished not with them that believed not, when she had received the spies with peace."
— Hebrews 11:31

The Counselor's Insight: The Stigma vs. The Strategy In my counseling practice, I see so many women who are paralyzed by their "starting point." They believe the label the world gave them—"The Addict," "The Divorcee," "The Failure"—is their permanent identity. Rahab was labeled "The Prostitute," but God saw "The Strategist." She had the discernment to recognize a move of God before anyone else in Jericho did.

Pastor Sheila's Reflection: The Dress Rehearsal My sisters, your past was just a dress rehearsal for your future. Rahab had to live on the wall to eventually become the one who helped tear the walls down. You have already paid the price for your mistakes; stop letting people charge you interest on a debt that God has already canceled.

- **Know Your Worth:** Never stay where you are merely tolerated. Pivot to where you are celebrated.

- **The Genealogy of Grace:**

- Rahab didn't just survive Jericho; she entered the bloodline of Jesus. Your "stain" doesn't disqualify you; it prepares you for the lineage of the miraculous.

Your Rahab-imitation: A Moment to Reflect

1. **The Label:** What is the "harlot label" or the "stain" that the world (or your own mind) has tried to pin on you?

____

____

____

____

____

____

----

2. **The Pivot:** Rahab chose to align with the Spies of Israel rather than the Kings of Jericho. What "old alliance" or toxic circle do you need to leave behind today to protect your future?

----

3. The Household Covenant: Rahab's faith saved her entire family. Who are you standing in the gap for today?

The Oxygen: A Prayer for the Woman on the Wall

"Lord, thank You that my starting point does not dictate my finish line. I thank You that You are the God of the second, third, and fourth chance. Today, I take off the label of my past and I put on the mantle of my purpose. I choose to be around those who celebrate the Grace on my life. I am Rahab-imitated by Your blood. In Jesus' Name, Amen."

A Woman of Courage: The Strategic Advance

Picture the woman with an issue of blood (Matthew 9:20-22) setting up her strategic advance on how she would get to the Master. She knew there would be interference with the haters and the mockers. She knew the level of warfare would be great.

After all her life had been a living Hell, but she needed to get to the King. Close your eyes now and say Lord let me touch the hem of your garment. The woman had an appetite that had to be. filled. She did not want a house, a job, a prayer for her mother or sister, she was hungry for deliverance and needed her healing. She heard many stories about the Lord, and her faith started to grow when she heard about HIM. Because when you are going through trials and hardship it is faith you need. Faith will push you, faith. will carry you through storms and disappointment. Faith speaks.

To crisis, faith brings deliverance. if you believe in the natural Eye, you will see trouble and your faith will be weakened, she refused to believe what the doctors said or what people said about her. It's Faith that will spring forth up in you let your Faith. Spring forth and like our sister with the issue of blood, she let Nothing stops her, she closed her ears to the nay Sayers and haters. Those that scorned her saw her get her deliverance. The Mockers and haters became her audience of envy.

What's Your Issue? Give it to the Master and Believe

The Hem and the Healed Heart: The Woman Whose Name is Known to God

"For she said within herself, If I may but touch his garment, I shall be whole." — Matthew 9:21

The Counselor's Insight: The Fatigue of the "Issue" In my counseling practice, I see women who have been "bleeding" for years—not always physically, but emotionally. They have a "stain" that won't stop draining them. Like this woman, they have "suffered many things of many physicians" and spent all they had, only to grow worse. This is the fatigue of the "Issue." It isolates you. It makes you feel "unclean" in your own skin. But healing doesn't start with the crowd; it starts with the *Inner Dialogue*. She said *within herself*, "I shall be whole."

Pastor Sheila's Reflection: The Power is in the Tassel

My sisters, we often say she touched the "hem," but my studies show she was reaching for something much more specific. She was reaching for the **Tzitzit**—the sacred tassels on the corners of Jesus's Tallit. The prophecy in Malachi 4:2 says the Sun of Righteousness shall arise with "healing in His wings." In Hebrew, the word for "wings" (*kanaph*) also means the "corners" or "edges" of a garment where the tassels hang.

She wasn't just grabbing a cloak; she was catching the **Covenant**. She didn't have a name recorded in the scrolls of men—her name is buried in the heart of God—but she had a *Touch* that stopped the Master in His tracks.

- **Interference vs. Intention:** There will always be "haters" and a "crowd" between you and your breakthrough. Don't let the noise of the crowd keep you from the Power in the Tassel.

- **The Invisible Name:** You may feel anonymous in your pain, but you are famous in His presence.

Touching the Tassel: A Moment to Reflect

1. The Drainage: What is the "Issue" that has been draining your joy, your peace, or your resources for "twelve years" (or a long season)?

----

2. The Inner Dialogue: What are you saying *within yourself* today? Are you saying "I am stained," or are you saying "If I may but touch, I shall be whole"?

3. The Push: What "crowd" of opinions or "interference" from your past do you need to push through to reach the hem of His garment?

The Oxygen: A Prayer for the Woman in the Crowd

"Lord, I am tired of the 'Issue' that has been draining my life. I stop looking to the 'physicians' of this world for what only You can do. Today, I pushed through the crowd of my fears, and I reach for the Tassel. I catch hold of Your Covenant and Your Word. I thank You that even if the world doesn't know my name, you know my heart. I am made whole by the Power in Your wings. In Jesus' Name, Amen."

The WINPOP Mandate: Women in Pursuit of Purpose

"For I know the thoughts that I think toward you, saith the Lord, thoughts of peace, and not of evil, to give you an expected end." — *Jeremiah 29:11*

The Counselor's Insight: The Center of Operation In my counseling practice, I often explain that the heart is the seat of the will, the intellect, and the emotions. It is the "Center of Operations" for your entire life. If your heart is still carrying the weight of a "Stain," your operations will be sluggish. To pursue your purpose, you must first permit your heart to be processed. As you move through these pages, remember: **When nothing changes, nothing changes.** Transformation requires a shift in your daily "Internal Dialogue."

Pastor Sheila's Reflection: The Beautiful Queen's Pursuit My sisters, you were born with a purpose to be all that God created you to be. You are a Queen who has surrendered her crown to the King of Kings. As you engage with Power **Words** and reflections in the pages ahead, I want you to share your most intimate feelings with the Father. Don't just read these words; let them beat with the rhythm of your own heart.

The Purpose-Driven Practice: 6 Keys to Your Transformation

1. **Write Your Vision:** Document your goals daily; a vision that isn't written is just a wish.

----

2. The Gratitude Log: Note three things you are grateful for every day. Gratitude is the enemy of the "Stain."

3.The Problem Transfer: Journal your problems, then consciously hand them to the "Ultimate Constructor."

4.Stress Release: Identify your stress so you can apply the "Oxygen of Grace" to them.

5.Listen to Learn: Practice being silent so you can hear the Lords specific instructions for your life.

----

6. The Power of Now: Be completely present at this moment. Today is the only day you have to start your pursuit.

Prayer for the Family

Heavenly Father teach us how to pray. help me find that quiet room to talk to you every day let us know when we are unable to utter a word. You are listening to our hearts and filling our souls and minds with your wisdom, knowledge, and perfect peace...Father, we want to walk and pray with You every day we love you with all our hearts, our soul and our mind. Strengthen our family cord that nothing can break it. Let's pray together so we can stay together. This is our humble prayer today. In Jesus Name We Pray.

Prayer

'WHEN NOTHING CHANGES,
NOTHING CHANGES'

Lord God, you are my king. You are my fortress, and in you I am safe and secure. I shall worship and praise your name. Thank you for providing for me daily. Thank you for being my healer.

Thank you for always being Faithful. Thank you for never leaving me nor forsaking me. Thank you for the wonderful things you have done and the miracles you have performed. Thank you, Lord for Peace.

In Jesus Name I Pray

Amen

I will exalt you; you are my God and my hiding place my safe refuge, most holy Father, you are my friend your always near you always come right on time.

23 Psalm (kjv)

The Lord is my shepherd; I shall not want.

2 He maketh me lie down in green pastures: he leadeth me beside the still waters.

3 He restoreth my soul: he leadeth me on the paths of righteousness for his name's sake.

4 Yea, though I walk through the valley of the shadow of death, I will fear no evil: for thou art with me; thy rod and thy staff they comfort me.

5 Thou preparest a table before me in the presence of mine enemies: thou anoint my head with oil; my cup runneth over.

6 Surely goodness and mercy shall follow me
all the days of my life: and I will dwell in the
house of the Lord forever.

Prayer

'WHEN NOTHING CHANGES, NOTHING CHANGES'

Lord Jesus thank you for waking me up this morning you are my hope, you are my peace, you are my life. Thank you, Lord, for loving me unconditionally. My great and mighty God I thank you for your loving kindness towards me no one can love me like you do. No one can understand me like you do you are my shield in the time of trouble. I desire to know you more and more. Lord

Jesus I adore you thank you for your love. In Jesus' name I pray

Amen

Prayer

'WHEN NOTHING CHANGES, NOTHING CHANGES'

Father, I rise to say good morning Holy Spirit I rise with the strength, power and knowledge and no weapon formed against me shall prosper you have given me the power to speak to the mountains to be moved, when I find myself in the valley you are there if I find myself on the mountaintop there you are with me. You have given me a spirit of Power, love, and a sound mind.

Today I WALK in victory I command this day to be favorable and successful in all that I do. Thank you, Lord.

Amen

Prayer

'WHEN NOTHING CHANGES, NOTHING CHANGES'

King of Glory, you are sovereign, and you are omnipresent. It is because of you that I live move and have my being. Thank you, Lord, for breathing the breath of life into me each day. We can do all we can to fulfill our purpose on the earth. I command and declare that this day shall be an amazing day. Yes, there are external things that attempt to distract us and disturb our peace, but we know that when we call on your great name demons flee, hell gets nervous and we your children are protected by you. Thank you, Father, for fighting for us and coming to our rescue, you are God and beside you there is no other. In Jesus Name I pray

Prayer

'WHEN NOTHING CHANGES,
NOTHING CHANGES'

Pray with me my sisters!

Good morning,

Let us come before our father quietly in prayer on this beautiful morning.

"But when you pray go into your room, close the door and pray to your Father who is unseen, then your Father, who sees what is done in secret, will reward you "

Matthew 6:6 NIV New International Version

Prayer

'WHEN NOTHING CHANGES, NOTHING CHANGES'

Heavenly Father teach us how to pray. help us find that quiet room to talk to you every day. Let us know when we are unable to utter a word, you are listening to our hearts and filling our souls and minds with your wisdom, knowledge, and perfect peace.

Father, I want to walk and pray with you every day. I love you with all my heart, soul, and mind. This is my prayer today. In

Jesus Precious and Holy Name, I pray.

Amen

Prayer

'WHEN NOTHING CHANGES, NOTHING CHANGES'

Lord Thank you for yet another day to rise and shine and give you Glory. As I start this new day let it me pleasing in your sight.

I know that it is by your Grace that I am able to not quit, every day is a day to push and achieve and strive to be a better me. I erase doubt and fear from my thoughts remembering that I can do all things through Christ who strengthens me. When things get rough, I pause and reflect on everything you brought me through, I pause and look at your creation like the morning dew, the sun and the dawn of the day, it's all the beauty of your holiness. I take the reins of my life and move forward in the authority you have given me pushing past all things that try to cancel my God given assignment. I am focused and ready for this day. Father thank you for your unconditional love. I give you all the Glory and Praise in the mighty name of Jesus. Be Glorified

Amen

Prayer

'WHEN NOTHING CHANGES, NOTHING CHANGES'

Father, thank you for this new day to acknowledge you, you are intentionally caring for me that I may remain in peace with myself and others. You have given your Angels charge over me.

Thank you for protecting me and my family, it is by your Grace that I can do all that I do. I will continue to give you Praise and realize that all things are possible with you. Thank you for

never forsaking me, thank you for your unconditional love even in times when I was not doing my best, you came through for me

with no condemning judgment. I thank you not for what you do but because of who you are. Thank you for a brand-new day.

In Jesus Name, Amen

Good morning, Holy Spirit, I thank you for my rise on this day. I have never seen this day before, but I rise with gratitude and humility giving you all the praise. I continue to look to the hills from which cometh my help, my help comes from the Lord who made heaven and earth. Awesome Ruler Mighty God thank you for the power and authority to tread over serpents. Thank you for the power of your word. There is no one like you. I know and believe that you are working everything out for my good. When I am happy you are near, when I am sad you are there, when I am sick you are there, when people turn their back on me, I will find you near. I am so grateful you call me, friend. Thank you, Lord, for catching every tear and turning my tear dops into showers of joy. I have learned from you how to trade my sorrows for the joy of the lord. There is no one like you I have searched all over and I found no one like you. Lord cover me and my family and friends today with the Power of your blood as I walk this day out. Walking in power and in victory.

In the mighty majestic name of Jesus.

**But they who wait for the Lord shall renew their strength; they shall mount up with wings like eagles they shall run and not be weary; they shall walk and not faint. **

The Power Word Treasury: Jewels for the Journey

"Finally, sisters, whatever is true, whatever is noble, whatever is right, whatever is pure, whatever is lovely, whatever is admirable—if anything is excellent or praiseworthy—think about such things." — Philippians 4:8

P — PASSIONATE

If you want to be passionate for God, you must let Him protect and defend you when the world criticizes your lavish love for Him. Don't defend yourself. Just love God; He will use your passion for His glory.

T — TRANSFORMING

God cleans us up by taking our sins away from our life and making us a new creature in Christ. But every day, He works on us to make us what we need to be for Him in this life.

W — WELLNESS

Do not be anxious about anything, but in everything by prayer and supplication with thanksgiving, let your request be known unto God. When the righteous cry for help, the Lord hears and delivers them out of all their troubles

W — WORTHY

Remember that the battle is the Lord's. David reminds us that our God is a God who is worthy to be worshiped! He is worthy of being our Delight, our Dependence, and our Devotion. He is worthy to be praised, exalted, and followed.

R — RADIANCE

Those who look to Him are radiant with joy; their faces will never be ashamed. *(Psalm 34:5)*

R — RENEWAL

They who wait on the Lord shall renew their strength. They shall mount up with wings like eagles; they shall run and not be weary; they shall walk and not faint.

P — PASSIONATE

If you want to be passionate for God, you must let Him protect and defend you when the world criticizes your lavish love for Him. Don't defend yourself. Just love God; He will use your passion for His glory.

W — WELLNESS

Do not be anxious about anything, but in everything by prayer and supplication with thanksgiving, let your request be known unto God. When the righteous cry for help, the Lord hears and delivers them out of all their troubles.

T — THRIVING

Will you progress towards your goals? Will you realize that despite circumstances, you have the strength to thrive?

P — PURPOSEFUL

I cry out to God Most High, to God who fulfills His purpose for me. This key is understanding God's purpose for your life. God has numbered your days and will fulfill every purpose He has for you. *(Psalm 57:2)*

E — EXUBERANT

The wage of a good person is exuberant life; an evil person ends up with nothing but sin. *(Proverbs 10:16)*

E — ENERGETIC

Be active; do not get weary. Energize your purpose by feeding your spirit with positivity. It will push you to that next place in your destiny.

B — BRILLIANCE

Having the glory of God, your radiance is like a most precious jewel, like a jasper, clear as crystal. You are seen and noticed in your brilliance.

A — ABUNDANCE

"More abundantly" means to have a super-abundance of a thing. Abundant life refers to life in its abounding fullness of joy and strength for the spirit, soul, and body.

A — ALIGN

Ask God to reveal the goals, dreams, and plans you should be pursuing that align with His will. Be quiet enough to hear His voice; if He gives you a big, audacious goal, trust Him to lead and guide you.

V — VISIONARY

Write the vision and make it plain. For still the vision awaits its appointed time; it hastens to the end. It will not lie. If it seems slow, wait for it; it will surely come.

L — LUMINOUS

Even in your darkest moments, your light is shining. You are a Luminous Queen.

C — CREATIVITY

Creativity is the act of turning new and imaginative ideas into reality. It is the ability to perceive the world in new ways and find hidden patterns. You can develop and express yourself in new ways.

D — DISCOVERY

Continue to discover who you are, Queen. The Lord says in His word: "Dear children, you are from God and have overcome them, because the one who is in you is greater than the one who is in the world."

R — RESULTS

Stop. Pause. Reflect. Sit still and be quiet. Think of the results you need to help you live out your purpose

A Letter to My Sisters in Pursuit of Purpose

My Dear Sister,

We are successful not because we are perfect, but because we are always striving. I want you to hold yourself accountable to the greatness God has placed within you. Don't just walk through these days—live them with intention. I am leaving you with these thoughts, not as a test, but as a mirror for your soul. Ponder these things as you move into your purpose:

- **What was your biggest priority this week?** Did you give your best to what matters most, and if not, what held you back?

- **What did you learn in the quiet moments?** Every week carries a lesson if we are still enough to hear it.

- **What was your biggest obstacle, and what do you need to solve it?** Remember, the obstacle isn't there to stop you; it's there to show you the strength you didn't know you had.

- **What was your biggest personal highlight?** Celebrate the "Kabod" moments, the small victories where you felt the father's hand.

- **What needs to happen to make next week a success?** And most importantly, what do you need help with, and who do you need to contact?

You don't have to carry the weight alone. Find those who will reassure you that your goals are manifesting. You are a Queen in pursuit of a divine purpose. Let the stain fade into the background of your victory.

With all my love, **Sheila P. Ingram**

I SEAL THE PRAYERS AND WORDS IN THIS BOOK WITH THE POWER OF CHRIST.... PASTOR SHEILA INGRAM

DEDICATIONS

THE MATRIARCH'S CROWN

(To Dorothy Lee "DeDe")

To my Mother:

Mommy, I could not be who I am today—I would not even be able to stand—if it wasn't for watching you stand through the stains and the struggles you had to rise above. In my heart, you were and are the strongest woman I have ever seen.

I watched you transition from what you called a "late bloomer" into a woman of stature, strength, power, and knowledge. Thank you for walking with me, even when you felt I had made a wrong turn. You never slighted me. You never turned your back on me. You never hung your head ashamed when you walked with me. Instead, you told all three of us: **"Pick your head up. Hold your head up when you walk."**

The Sacred Exchange: It must be noted that while I was carrying my youngest daughter, the Lord weas about to take you home preparing.

You never got to meet her, but her very existence is a tribute to your life. I named her **De Anjolie"** to ensure your name and my father's name would never be forgotten. I took your name, **DeDe (Dorothy Lee)**, and my father's name, **Joe**, and connected them together to create her identity.

Though you both transitioned so close in time—Daddy and Mommy, you left me with a living legacy. Every time I call her name, I am calling yours. I know you are smiling down on us. I am finally released from the things that held me. Because of your strength, **I can fly now. I am free now.** Thank you, Mommy. I love you eternally.

To my Father, James Ingram

Thank you for the foundation. You provided the roots from which I grew, and even in the quiet spaces, your influence remained. I honor the Ingram name that you gave me—a name that became a "Singer's Standard" in Harlem and across the world, a "Pulpit Authority" across the nations, and a "Manual of Healing" in this very book.

I carry your strength and your name with pride, and I hope I have added glory to the lineage you started. I love you

THE COVENANT KEEPERS

To My Chosen Circle:

While there are many who have crossed my path, there are a few who stood as pillars when the building was falling.

To Diane Bailey: You are the definition of a Covenant Sister. When the doors closed and the crowds thinned, you stayed. You fed me, tended to me, and loved me when I felt unlovable.

To Pat Finney: You have been a silent rock in my life, the Godmother to my youngest, you have been the safe haven of love. Thank You

To Deaconess Roslyn Spriggs: What a jewel you are. Your love has been a constant, unconditional anchor in my life.

To Dr. Denise Robinson: Your unconditional love carries me a very long way, your kindness remains a constant memory, Thank you for our unbreakable sisterhood and constant laughter.

To Kathy: Thank you for the sisterhood, the kindness, and strength, and the way we can act silly and laugh like little carefree schoolgirls. You have a heart of gold. Thank you for sharing your mother with me.

To Sandra Birthright: Thank you for your love and for being you. Thank you for the laughter. You are a jewel, and I love you dearly.

To Patricia Finney, thank you for your unconditional love you were my village when I had none, you poured into Dee as if she was your own. You are an incredible woman with a huge heart. Thank You.

To Deborah aka Peaches, thank you for listening to the Lord and coming to take me to church. Thank you for being a lifetime friend may God continue to Bless you.

To the many others who carried me when I couldn't carry myself: Your names are etched in my heart

SACRED DEDICATION (The Spiritual Foundations)

To my Spiritual Mothers, now home with the Lord:

To Mother Irma McLeod: When my mother, Dorothy, went home to the Lord, I was left empty. But God, in His infinite mercy, etched you into my life. You became my mother in every sense of the word. You stuck with me through the thick and the thin; you prayed me through and influenced the woman I am today. I miss you greatly.

To Apostle Karen Veney-Register: Thank you for being the prophetic voice that sought me out while you were in Amsterdam. You became my covering and spoke life into my destiny. Though you are now home with the Master, your mantle remains.

A Tribute to Dr. Ernest Cameron: To the man who raised me up in the Word: Thank you, Dr. Ernest Cameron. You taught me the unadulterated Word of God. You Ordained me and told me that I was born to sing and born to speak. I honor your investment in my life and the rock-solid foundation you laid for my ministry.

A MOTHER'S BLESSING

To my Daughters, Nichole, Pache' and DeAnjolie'

It is the highest honor of my life that God allowed me to be your mom. I love you with eternal love, and I know the best is yet to come for your lives. Continue to grow, to love, and to serve the Master with your whole hearts. When you find yourselves hitting a wall, remember that He is near. **Hold your heads up.** Your grandmother's command is now your inheritance.

To my youngest, De Anjolie'

I must give you a special thank you for that prophetic moment in the restaurant in California. As we were having our heart-to-heart about the family, you were sensitive to the Spirit. God used your words and that whole prophetic illustration of the **Stain** to birth the revelation of this book.

It was through your vessel that the word **"The Stain"** was released into the atmosphere. Because of your obedience at that moment, what began as a talk about our family has now become a **Manual of Restoration** and a global movement for **"A Heart Without Walls."** We are erasing the stain for women and men across the globe. Thank you for being sensitive to that heart-to-heart moment. This word was birthed through your heart, and for that, I am eternally grateful.

THE INGRAM LINEAGE (Roots and Wings)

To my brother, Edward Ingram: Thank you for supporting everything I have ever done. You have been there to root me on every stage, through every trial. You are my only brother—continue to rise and be the best version of yourself. I love you.

To my sister, Linda: Though you are home with the Lord, your impact remains. Thank you for helping me when I couldn't help myself. Thank you for the love you poured into my children. You are truly missed.

To Carol: Thank you for being "Tailored Made" for my brother and for being a pillar in our family. Thank you for your kindness, your strength, and for being the "family doctor." Continue to be quiet in spirit but strong in your walk.

TO MY SPIRITUAL DAUGHTERS AND SONS

To my spiritual daughters and my spiritual sons: You know who you are. Thank you. Thank you so much for trusting me with your lives and for honoring me as your spiritual mother. Thank you for letting my voice be a sounding board as you gathered the jewels from my journey to build your own.

Continue to press and lean into God. Continue to stand tall and know exactly who you are in Him. Remember my heart for you: When nothing changes, nothing changes. So, whatever you do, keep moving. I love you all unconditionally.

THE GLOBAL COVENANT

(The Nations)

To the Sisters of the Nations: My heart has been knitted with women of different languages and cultures across the globe. To those who loved me, rooted for me, and prayed me through—thank you.

To the Bishops, Apostles, and Leaders: Thank you for embracing me and inviting me from the United States to your pulpits to preach, to sing, and to usher in the Presence of God. Special Thanks to Bishop Vasale, you held me up when all Hell was breaking loose in my life, you have an amazing heart. Thank you. Apostle Victor Mebele and Pastor Liselore you are my dear friends thank you for your continued support. To Apostle David Durant thank you for the years that you covered me and the times we flowed in the Spirit.

To Eugene Huybregts and First Lady Solange, You were the first on the island of Curacao to open the door, allowing God to cause me to "breathe" on that island. Your faith in my mantle changed my trajectory. Thank you

Let Music Play

Don Hamilton: You have been a blessing to my life and career, you made it easy for me to perform with confidence as my musical director of Vocals, you are my lifetime friend and I love you, you are special Don Hamilton

Reggie Segar's Although you are not here, I feel your spirit and push to never stop singing. You were the one who built my confidence and reinforced me over and over that I had a beautiful voice and I could rise with a career, every rehearsal you pushed my vocal ability. You were family and I miss you tremendously. I could use one of those talks right about now. But I will close my eyes and hear your voice of encouragement.

To every background singer and band member we did it, to sold out audiences, It's because of you all showing up every time I had a Gig that I was able to perform in excellence, we became a team and family thank you for your continued support for all of the years we grace the stage together. Love you all. YOU ROCK !!

TO THE QUEENS & KINGS (Nieces & Nephews)

To my Nieces and Great Nieces: I speak from my heart to yours. Thank you for becoming the beautiful Queens that you are. Never allow anyone to cause you to "power down." When you walk into a room, let your light shine. You were designed for this day and for your position.

To my Nephews: You all are wonderful, and I love you so much. Even though our family is female top-heavy, you stand out in your own right. Continue to be the men God has called you to be. Reach deep into the heart of the Father to find your purpose and your path.

THE HARVEST (Grandchildren & Great-Grandchild)

To my Grandchildren—Chad, Destiny, Pache', Sir, Amia, Eden and my Great-Grandchild, Liam:

I love you eternally. My prayer for you is simple: **Lean into God.** Just lean into Him, and He will always be there to meet you. Grow strong, walk heavy in your purpose, and never shrink back from all God has called you to be. Remember: **It's not how you start; it's how you finish.**

THE GENERATIONAL BRIDGE

(To the Seeds Unborn)

To the Generations Yet to Come:

Life will deal you hands that you think you cannot play. People may try to download lies into your spirit, but I want you to stand on God's Word. You are part of my seed and my legacy; that means you are built to survive and designed to soar. When you feel stuck, remember: **When nothing changes, nothing changes. So, keep it movin'.** I may not see the places you go, but I know you will get there because of the strength of this lineage. I Love You

THE STAGE, THE PULPIT, & THE COUCH (The Credits)

THE INTERNATIONAL ARTIST & SCREENWRITER

My voice has been my passport. From the **Apollo Theater** and **Lincoln Center** to living and performing in **Italy**, I have shared the spotlight with the greats like **Lou Rawls Johnny Mathis, Nancy Wilson, Helen Baylor, The Clark Sisters, Donnie McKurklin and so many others.**

 As a songwriter, I have penned over **35 to 40 original songs**. Today, my pen continues to move as a **Screenwriter**, developing scripts that bring the "Faded Stain" from the page to the screen through **Ingram Restoration Global LLC.**

THE HARLEM PILLAR & COMMUNITY MARSHAL

My heart belongs to the streets that raised me. I served as the **Grand Marshal of Harlem,** leading massive outreaches in every major Harlem park for years. From feeding the homeless to reuniting families and helping our youth navigate the struggles of school and life, I have been a frontline general in community restoration. For over five years, I led dedicated outreaches to the homeless, proving that no one is beyond the reach of a "Heart Without Walls."

THE GLOBAL MINISTER & DIGITAL BROADCASTER

For 38 years, I have carried a mantle of restoration. Through **Women in Pursuit of Purpose (WINPOP),** I have hosted decades of annual conferences that have touched thousands of women in the U.S. and internationally.

Today, I am building the future through my two YouTube networks: **The Sheila Ingram Ministry Network** and the **Bravo with Sheila Network**. These platforms were built from the ground up to provide a 24/7 digital sanctuary for those seeking "Erase the Stain" revelation and professional guidance.

THE CREDENTIALED CLINICIAN

Behind every outreach is the expertise of a **Licensed Professional Counselor (LPC)**. Specializing in **Temperament Counseling** and **CBT**, my clinical practice is the bridge between spiritual deliverance and mental wholeness. I didn't just survive the trenches; I became the architect of their restoration.

PASTOR SHEILA INGRAM, LPC, Doctorate (Cand.)

A Licensed Professional Counselor (LPC) and a veteran of the Gospel for over 38 years, Sheila Ingram holds a **Master of Ministry** and is currently a **Doctoral Candidate**.

FOR BOOKING, SPEAKING, & CLINICAL COUNSELING: To bring the message of "The Faded Stain" and "A Heart Without Walls" to your city, church, or organization, please contact our executive office:

- **Email:** Sheila@IngramRestoration.com
- **Primary Business Line:** 352-695-0771
- **Executive Line:** 917-325-0292

INGRAM RESTORATION GLOBAL LLC

- **Website:** www.Ingramrestoration.com

INGRAM RESTORATION GLOBAL OUTREACH INC.

- **Website:** www.IRGOUTREACH.ORG

DIGITAL NETWORKS:

- **YouTube:** The Sheila Ingram Ministry Network
- **YouTube:** Bravo with Sheila Network

THE RESTORATION INDEX
(Scriptural Anchors)

. Here are 25 powerful scriptures to anchor the "Faded Stain."

On Forgiveness & The Faded Stain:

1. **Isaiah 1:18:** "Though your sins be as scarlet, they shall be as white as snow."

2. **Psalm 103:12:** "As far as the east is from the west, so far has He removed our transgressions from us."

3. **Micah 7:19:** "You will cast all our sins into the depths of the sea."

4. **Hebrews 8:12:** "Their sins and their lawless deeds I will remember no more."

5. **2 Corinthians 5:17:** "Therefore, if anyone is in Christ, he is a new creature; old things are passed away..."

On Strength & "Harlem Tough" Resilience:

6. **Isaiah 40:31:** "But those who wait on the Lord shall renew their strength; they shall mount up with wings like eagles."

7. **Philippians 4:13:** "I can do all things through Christ who strengthens me."

8. **Joshua 1:9:** "Be strong and of good courage; do not be afraid... for the Lord your God is with you."

9. **2 Timothy 1:7:** "For God has not given us a spirit of fear, but of power and of love and of a sound mind."

10. **Psalm 18:2:** "The Lord is my rock and my fortress and my deliverer."

On Restoration & The "Erase the Stain" Movement:

11. **Joel 2:25:** "I will restore to you the years that the swarming locust has eaten."

12. **1 Peter 5:10:** "After you have suffered a while, [He will] perfect, establish, strengthen, and settle you."

13. **Jeremiah 30:17:** "For I will restore health to you and heal you of your wounds, says the Lord."

14. **Isaiah 61:3:** "To give them beauty for ashes, the oil of joy for mourning."

15. **Job 42:10:** "And the Lord restored Job's losses... the Lord gave Job twice as much as he had before."

On A Heart Without Walls (Identity & Peace):

16. **Proverbs 4:23:** "Keep your heart with all diligence, for out of it spring the issues of life."

17. **Psalm 34:18:** "The Lord is near to those who have a broken heart."

18. **Ezekiel 36:26:** "I will give you a new heart and put a new spirit within you."

19. **John 14:27:** "Peace I leave with you, My peace I give to you."

20. **Romans 8:37:** "In all these things we are more than conquerors through Him who loved us."

On The Finish Line:

21. **Philippians 1:6:** "He who has begun a good work in you will complete it."

22. **Galatians 6:9:** "And let us not grow weary while doing good, for in due season we shall reap if we do not lose heart."

23. **2 Timothy 4:7:** "I have fought the good fight, I have finished the race, I have kept the faith."

24. **Habakkuk 2:2:** "Write the vision and make it plain on tablets."

25. **Psalm 138:8:** "The Lord will perfect that which concerns me."

e Greate   em
hamber of   merce
ished in 18

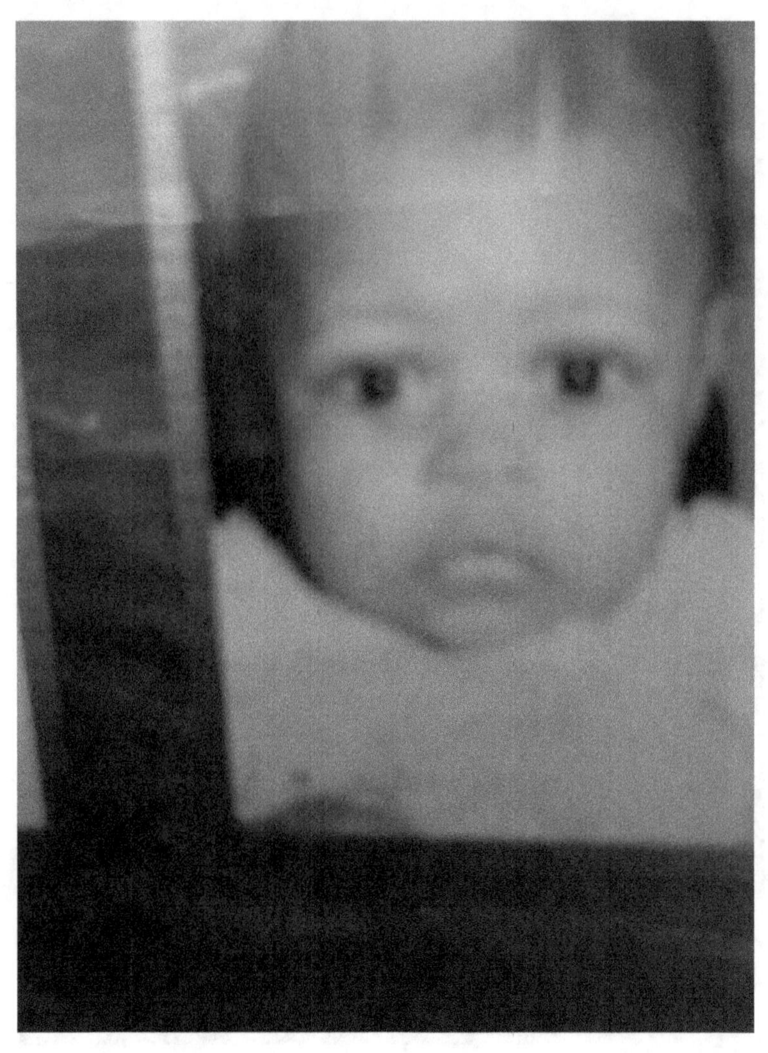

12 45

"ITS NOT HOW YOU START ITS
HOW YOU FINISH"

12 45™

KEEP IT MOVON !!

"HEART WITHOUT WALLS"
ERASING THE STAIN

SHINE-A-LIGHT21
Annual Mother's Day Event
ry Of
ngram

NATIONAL EMERGENCY RESOURCES:

If you are in crisis or need immediate support as you navigate your own restoration, please reach out to these professional services:

- **National Suicide Prevention Lifeline:** 988
- **National Domestic Violence Hotline:** 1-800-799-SAFE (7233)
- **SAMHSA National Helpline (Substance Abuse):** 1-800-662-HELP (4357)
- **Crisis Text Line:** Text HOME to 741741